Success in Higher Modern Studies

Frank Cooney
John McTaggart

ACKNOWLEDGEMENTS

The authors and publishers would like to thank Paul Creaney for his contribution to this text.

Published and typeset by
Pulse Publications
Braehead, Stewarton Road,
by Kilmaurs, Ayrshire
KA3 2NH

Printed and bound by
Thomson Colour Printers

British Library Cataloguing-in-Publication Data
A Catalogue record for this book is available from the British Library

ISBN 1 905817 02 9
© Pulse Publications/ModernityScotland

CONTENTS

A

Decision Making in Scotland

Reference to the Pulse Publications textbook *UK Politics Today*, Chapters 8, 9 and 10 and www.modernityscotland.com will enhance the use of these revision notes. It is assumed that you have studied the course and have a sound understanding of the key political issues in the UK.

EXAM REQUIREMENTS

You are expected to display knowledge and understanding of:

1. Decision making in Scotland: the Scottish Parliament as an arena for conflict, cooperation and decision making; functions; organisation of and procedures for business. The Scottish Executive; the respective roles of the First Minister and the Cabinet. The effects of the electoral system on decision making for Scotland at Holyrood level.

2. Representation of Scottish interests at Westminster. The distribution of powers between the Scottish Parliament and the UK Parliament; cooperation and conflict between the Scottish Parliament and Scottish Executive and the UK Parliament. The effects of the electoral system on Westminster decision making for Scotland.

3. Local government in Scotland: role, functions, finance and reform. COSLA, cooperation and conflict with the Scottish Executive. The effects of the electoral system on local authority decision making.

Key issue:
To what extent do local authorities cooperate with the Scottish Parliament?

Scottish local government has been the subject of a great deal of change in recent times. It was only in 1996 that the present thirty two local authorities were created, many of them controversially.

Local authorities jealously guard the services they are responsible for. They take great pride in the 'quality and value of service' they offer, often comparing these with neighbouring authorities. These are the services which impact greatly on our lives:

- our schools;
- our parks;
- our roads;
- our houses;
- our refuse collection;
- our libraries.

Scottish people pay a special tax to the local authority, the Council Tax, for these services so voters expect a great deal, or 'best value' in return for the payment of Council Tax.

The Scottish Parliament assumed control of local government as part of the devolution settlement. It also became responsible for major services such as education and housing. The Scottish Executive has been very keen to see improvements in these services. It

has sought 'modernisation' of many old ways of working. But, in many cases, the Scottish Executive is dependent on local authorities on the ground to deliver change.

It is surely no accident, then, that the full title of the Scottish Executive Minister responsible for local government is The Minister for Finance and Public Service Reform.

The old relationships between local and central government will change.
As Labour is dominant in both the Scottish Parliament and local government, and since many Labour MSPs are former councillors, relations between the two bodies could be quite amicable. However, this is not always the case.

Why do tensions exist between Scottish local authorities and the Scottish Parliament?

The Scottish Parliament has struggled with its public image. Public disaffection, mostly about the cost of the building, has led many people to ask, "what is the point of the Parliament? What has it done for me?" Ministers, therefore, are under pressure not only to make a difference, but for the Scottish Parliament to be seen to be making a difference.

There are clear signs that the Scottish Executive is moving into treasured local government territory. If the Scottish Executive feels a local authority is not delivering services well enough, it can take it over. In June 2005, Inverclyde Council was the first Scottish council to find itself under the close scrutiny of the Scottish Executive following the publication of a poor inspection report by Audit Scotland. The authority was obliged to work with with a team of specialist officials from the Scottish Executive to improve its systems for delivering services to the people of Inverclyde.

Further reform of the traditional role of Scottish local authorities in key areas might be expected.

EDUCATION

Scottish local authorities jealously guard their historic role as providers of education. Yet many of the major initiatives are Scottish Executive, rather than local authority, driven. *Ambitious Excellent Schools, A Curriculum for Excellence* and *Determined to Succeed* are all initiatives from the Scottish Executive. The thirty two local authorities are expected to put these fresh approaches into practice. The Scottish Executive's team of Inspectors (HMIE) will inspect schools to see that progress is being made.

SOCIAL WORK

In 2003, Caleb Ness, a baby boy in Edinburgh whose parents were drug addicts, died. The City of Edinburgh Social Work Department accepted that mistakes had been made in its care of Caleb. First Minister Jack McConnell was furious and threatened to take action should the local authority social work department fail to improve its performance. City of Edinburgh Council has since completely reorganised its social work department, integrating it with other services into a new Children and Families Department.

CRIME

First Minister Jack McConnell is keen that local authorities should use Antisocial Behaviour Orders (ASBOs). Councils have been given the power to impose ASBOs on children under the age of 16 who have committed nuisance crimes as part of Justice Minister Cathie Jamieson's 'war on neds'.

The First Minister has championed ASBOs as a means of punishing individuals who cause chaos in the community. The orders allow courts to place restrictions on individuals, such as banning them from certain areas or from approaching certain people. In October 2004, under the *Antisocial Behaviour Act*, ASBOs were extended to 12 to 15-year-olds.

The problem of antisocial behaviour varies between Scotland's local authorities. Central Scotland, which includes Clackmannanshire, Falkirk and Stirling Councils witnessed, some of the country's worst examples of 'ned culture' over 2005 and 2006.

In October 2005, the First Minister called for local authorities to distribute leaflets naming and shaming those who had been served with an ASBO. Jack McConnell is concerned that some local authority leaders doubt that this will work. Some local authorities use ASBOs much more than others.

In 2003–04, the highest ASBO rates in Scotland were recorded in Dundee, Orkney, North Lanarkshire and Scottish Borders. This does not necessarily mean that these councils have more people committing nuisance crimes than other parts of Scotland, only that these local authorities are more likely to use ASBOs to deal with the problem.

Some local authorities feel that ASBOs interfere with the work of social workers to support families. By October 2005, Glasgow City Council, for example, had only ever used sixteen ASBOs. The Scottish Executive would like to see a more consistent use of ASBOs across the whole country.

TRANSPORT

As our roads fill up and global warming increases, transport policy is becoming an important issue for urban local authorities. In 2005, Edinburgh City Council held a referendum on whether to introduce charges on vehicles entering the city's boundaries.

To date, the Scottish Executive has done nothing to resolve the issue of road charging, but as the number of cars on the roads and the resultant traffic jams increase, it may well take action in the future.

The Scottish Executive has suggested plans to introduce a new National Transport Agency, which would try to integrate and improve air, road, rail and ferry services across the country.

Scottish Executive First Minister, Jack McConnell, meets with a representative of West Dunbartonshire Council to discuss tolls on the Erskine Bridge. The Council wants the tolls abolished but this can only be done by the Executive.

This has infuriated, amongst others, the Strathclyde Passenger Transport Authority (SPTA) which is an association of twelve West of Scotland local authorities and is the biggest UK transport organisation outside London. It sees transport as its responsibility, not that of the Executive.

HOUSING AND REGENERATION

Housing is one of local government's most important services. Per head of the population, Scotland has more people living in council housing than any other part of the UK.

In 1980 the Conservative government passed the *Housing Act* which enabled councils to sell their housing stock to sitting tenants. Limits were imposed on council house building. Since then there has been an increasing shortage of affordable homes for those who cannot afford to buy.

The Housing and Regeneration Agency (HRA) replaced Scottish Homes in 2001. Its role is to ensure decent housing and strong communities in Scotland. However, because the HRA is controlled by the Scottish Executive, some local councillors see it as a 'trojan horse', planning to move into new areas beyond housing and take power away from local authorities.

In 2003, Glasgow City Council tenants voted to set up a new Glasgow Housing Association (GHA). This new housing association does not make a profit, but it does not have  the same responsibilities as the local authority used to have. It can, unlike the former city council landlord, evict tenants for antisocial behaviour or non-payment of rent. In 2005, Edinburgh City Council tenants voted not to set up a similar housing association.

Some believe the future is bleak for local authorities in the areas of housing and education. They believe the years to come will see the big departments, such as education and housing, being centralised with the Scottish Executive, while local government is reduced to 'looking after parks and wheelie bins'.

MORE JOINED UP GOVERNMENT?

This is happening at a time when most of the Scottish Executive and the leadership of Scottish local authorities are members of the same political party. What tensions could arise if, say, the SNP or the Conservatives gained control of more local authorities? The introduction of the Single Transferable Vote (STV) in local government elections from 2007 could make conflict even more likely.

Further reform of Scottish local government is a distinct possibility. Many voters in Scotland remain confused over who provides services and who is responsible when things go wrong. Is it the local council or is it the Scottish Executive which is responsible?

Many people also feel that we are overgoverned. The average Scottish voter has a local councillor, an MP, eight MSPs and an MEP to represent him/her.

Pressure from England to reduce the amount of money the Scottish Parliament receives via the Barnett formula is likely to add to calls for local government to be more efficient in its provision of services.

This could lead to a reduction in the number of councils. For example, Council Tax payers in Ayrshire belong to one of three neighbouring local authorities North Ayrshire, South Ayrshire and East Ayrshire. Critics of the current arrangements point out that managing these small authorities involves unnecessary duplication of resources. Could bulk savings and best value be obtained through one large Ayrshire authority? Others point out that neighbouring local authorities could work together more to obtain savings, rather than working in isolation.

The Scottish Parliament refers to all the MSPs, together with the parliament's rules, powers and structures. The Scottish Parliament has its home at Holyrood in Edinburgh, although its committees often meet around the country.

However, the Scottish Executive is, in reality, where decisions are actually made. The Scottish Executive is composed of a coalition of leading Labour and Liberal Democrat MSPs. (This came about because no one party won an overall majority in the Scottish Parliament election.) The First Minister, normally the leader of the party with the largest number of MSPs, is elected by all members of the Scottish Parliament. S/He then appoints the other members of the Executive. The Scottish Executive is the devolved government for Scotland. It is responsible for most of the issues of day-to-day concern to the people of Scotland, including health, education, justice, rural affairs and transport. The Scottish Executive's main offices are at Victoria Quay, Edinburgh.

The Scottish Executive's Programme for Government is set out in the 2003 Partnership Agreement drawn up by the Scottish Labour and Scottish Liberal Democrat Parties.

Opposition MSPs can make a contribution to debates and discussions and because of the committee system and the greater time the Scottish Parliament allocates to Private Bills, backbench MSPs can have a greater impact than at Westminster. Nevertheless, the Scottish Executive remains the driving force behind the Scottish Parliament.

There have been demands to curb the powers of Scottish MPs at Westminster and to resolve, once and for all, the 'West Lothian Question'. (See page 7.)

If the Conservatives form the next Westminster government, they have promised to bar Scottish MPs from voting on 'English' issues. The increased level of ten-sion between Scotland and England may thwart Gordon Brown's ambitions to become Prime Minister. The English may well accept a Scottish Prime Minister, but perhaps not one who represents a Scottish constituency, and can vote on 'English' issues whilst English MPs cannot vote on issues devolved to the Scottish Parliament.

With Labour being in power at both Westminster and Holyrood, relations between the two Parliaments have been relatively good. However, what would happen if there was a Conservative victory at the next Westminster election? What would happen if there was an SNP/Green coalition committed to independence at the next Scottish Parliament election?

Already, there have been issues, especially those relating to immigration, which have tested the relations between the two parliaments in spite of there being a Labour First Minister and a Labour Home Secretary.

What are the Scottish Parliament's powers?

Even though there is now a Scottish Parliament, Scotland is not an independent country. It is not a 'sovereign' nation, with control over its own borders and the protection of those borders. Scotland remains part of the United Kingdom of Scotland, England, Wales and Northern Ireland. People entitled to live in Scotland are citizens of the United Kingdom. As evidence of this, when a new Scottish Parliament opens, the newly elected MSPs swear allegiance to the Queen. This has become the focus of protest by Scottish Socialist and SNP MSPs.

As at Westminster, all Bills passed by the Scottish Parliament have to receive the Royal Assent by the monarch before they can become law.

The Scottish Parliament manages an annual budget of around £27 billion. The Scottish Parliament has the power to vary the basic rate of income tax (22p in the pound in 2007) in Scotland by up to 3p in the pound. If elected to power, the SNP has announced plans to cut the basic rate of income tax.

To help make devolution work, a distinction has been made between powers which the UK Parliament in Westminster has retained and the powers which have been devolved to Scotland at Holyrood. Hence, we speak of the 'devolved' powers which the Scottish Parliament has and the 'reserved' powers which Westminster has.

Devolved Powers (Holyrood)

Health, education and training, local government, social work, housing, economic development, many aspects of transport, law and home affairs (including the police and the emergency services), the environment, agriculture, forestry and fishing, sport and the arts, statistics, public registers and records, tax varying powers of up to 3p in the pound.

Reserved powers (Westminster)

The constitution, UK foreign policy, UK defence and national security, UK fiscal, economic and monetary policy, immigration and nationality, employment legislation, social security, transport safety and regulation, various other powers including abortion, equal opportunities legislation and the National Lottery.

ACTION BY THE SCOTTISH PARLIAMENT

Since 1999, the Scottish Parliament has made a number of changes. These measures did not apply in England, although a smoking ban will be introduced in summer 2007.

Free personal care for the elderly

In 2002, the Scottish Executive took the decision to introduce free personal care for all elderly people in Scotland. This was a bold move and one which showed a 'Scottish' rather than a British approach to social policy.

No upfront tuition fees

Scottish students at Scottish universities do not pay their tuition fees until they graduate and earn a graduate level salary. Furthermore, unlike England there are no 'top-up' fees to be paid on popular courses. However, the row over tuition fees will not go away.

Controversially, in July 2005 the Scottish Executive imposed a 42% increase in fees for English students who come to Scottish universities, provoking claims of unfair discrimination. This decision was made in an attempt to reduce the number of so-called 'fee refugees'—English students who have headed to Scotland for their university education in order to avoid paying higher fees.

Ban on Smoking in Public Places

On 26 March 2006, the Scottish Parliament's ban on smoking in enclosed public places came into effect.

Free Bus Scheme

Elderly people in Scotland are now entitled to free travel by bus anywhere in the country.

In 2004–2005, the Scottish Parliament passed seventeen Bills which have received the Royal Assent and become Acts of the Scottish Parliament.

These have included The Education (Additional Support for Learning) Act, The Gaelic Language Act, The Antisocial Behaviour Act, The Breastfeeding Act, The National Health Service Reform Act.

DEVOLUTION OR INDEPENDENCE

Those who support the existing powers of the Scottish Parliament, such as Labour and the Liberal Democrats, believe these powers strike the right balance between solving issues which need specific Scottish solutions and those which the UK as a whole is better able to deal with.

Nationalists would like Scotland to be completely independent from the UK.

Before the Scottish Parliament was set up the Conservatives opposed it. However, the Party is now committed to its success, but remains opposed to independence.

Relations between Holyrood and Westminster

Three obvious sources of conflict are in funding, reserved powers and, as a consequence of this, the role of Scottish MPs at Westminster.

Taxation and Representation

Many English voters are becoming concerned at the devolved political settlement. As the Shadow Scottish Secretary, James Gray said,
> "Why should Scottish MPs be coming down to England and bossing us around?"

English voters are growing increasingly resentful that:
- the Scots, via the Barnett formula, are being given more taxpayers' money than the English and
- Scottish MPs can decide on 'English' matters, while English MPs have no say over many, now devolved, 'Scottish' matters.

The Scottish Parliament is funded by Westminster through the Barnett formula. Because of this formula, which was devised by a Labour Peer, Lord Barnett, in the 1970s, more money per head is spent by Westminster on Scotland than on other parts of the UK. This is because Scotland in those days was losing many of its traditional industries. The UK government of the day offered more money to help people in the communities suffering from the effects of high unemployment.

However, this is no longer the case. Parts of England, the north-east and north-west especially, are arguably worse off than many parts of Scotland. They do not receive special attention or funds.

One group, the English Democrats, led by tabloid journalist Gary Bushell, wants England to devolve from the rest of the UK. The English Democrats gained 130,000 votes at the 2005 general election.

The West Lothian Question

In terms of political representation, no one has properly answered the classic 'West Lothian Question':

> "Why should an MP from Blackburn in West Lothian be able to vote in the House of Commons on health issues which do not affect his constituents but have an impact on the constituents in Blackburn, England, but the MP for Blackburn in England cannot vote on health matters relating to Scotland?"

Tam Dalyell

The above question was posed by the Labour MP for Linlithgow at the time, Tam Dalyell, back in the 1970s when devolution first became a political issue. Dalyell, who was opposed to the setting up of a Scottish Parliament, claimed there was an injustice because Scottish MPs at Westminster would be able to make crucial decisions on issues which did not affect the voters they were representing.

The SNP has raised this contradiction to support the case for Scottish independence. The answer to the problem for the SNP is to separate the two parliaments completely.

Conservative leader David Cameron supports barring Scottish MPs, who tend to be Labour, from voting on 'English' issues in the Commons.

Two controversial issues have raised political temperatures. The first one was Scottish Labour MPs voting for Foundation Hospitals in England. *The Foundation Hospitals Bill* did not affect Scotland as health is a devolved matter. The Scottish Executive has no plans to introduce Foundation Hospitals. Opponents pointed to the fact that Tony Blair would have lost the vote if forty four Labour MPs from Scottish constituencies had not voted with the government.

A similar situation occurred during the Commons vote on university top-up tuition fees, also an issue which only affects English universities. Again, Tony Blair's Bill was saved only by the votes of Labour MPs from Scotland.

MPs from England have no opportunity to vote on health or education bills affecting Scotland as these are both devolved powers.

Immigration

Immigration is a reserved Westminster power. The Scottish Parliament cannot make decisions on who, or how many people can enter Scotland. That is a matter for the UK government, or more specifically the Home Secretary, to decide.

Immigration, however, is a complex business. The UK accepts into the country people who believe their life would be under threat if they remained in their own country. Such people are labelled 'asylum seekers' because they seek political asylum in the UK.

Immigration is a highly charged and emotive issue. Although the decisions about asylum applications are made by the UK government, the children of asylum seeking families will often be housed in Scottish local authority accommodation and go to Scottish schools. They will be cared for by the social work department of the Scottish local authority where they live.

These arrangements have been agreed between Scottish local authorities and the Home Office. In 2005, the case of the Vucaj family brought the issue of immigration to public attention.

The Vucaj family were asylum seekers from Albania. Because of the Balkans conflict in the early 1990s, they claimed that their lives would be at risk if they returned to Albania. They wished to live in Scotland on a permanent basis and applied for political asylum. The family lived in Glasgow for five years while their application for asylum was considered by the UK Home Office. The Vucaj family settled very well in Glasgow and the three children were very popular and successful pupils at a secondary school in Glasgow. The family's application was ultimately refused. In 2005, the media reported that the family had been taken from their home in Glasgow early in the morning by a deportation team from the UK Home Office. They were taken to England from where they were flown to Albania.

Supporters of the family alleged that their treatment had been 'inhumane'. It was distressing for the whole family, especially the children, to be woken at dawn and then physically removed from their home.

The issue clearly concerned First Minister Jack McConnell. It was not his decision to remove the family as he does not have this power. The Scottish Executive cannot change the law over immigration any more than it can change the law on pensions or interest rates. Nevertheless, the Vucajs were a family living in Scotland and being looked after by a Scottish local authority. It has been agreed that in future there will be a 'protocol' over the removal of failed asylum seekers between the UK Home Office and the Scottish Executive.

Study Theme 1B
Decision Making in Central Government

Reference to the Pulse Publications textbook *UK Politics Today*, Chapters 5, 6 and 7 and www.modernityscotland.com will enhance the use of these revision notes. It is assumed that you have studied the course and have a sound understanding of the key political issues in the UK.

EXAM REQUIREMENTS

You are expected to display knowledge and understanding of:

1 The Executive; the respective roles of the Prime Minister and Cabinet; accountability to Parliament; the role of senior civil servants in the UK political system.

2 Parliament (House of Commons and House of Lords) as an arena for conflict, cooperation and decision making; functions; organisation of and procedures for business.

3 Influences on the decision making process in the UK: the extent of these pressures, their impact and legitimacy.

Key issue:
To what extent can Parliament control the Executive?

To understand this issue, it is important to understand the relative powers of individuals and institutions in British politics.

At the outside of the power circle are members of the House of Lords. The House of Lords, while not powerless, is the least powerful of Parliament's institutions.

In the next layer are Opposition MPs. Opposition MPs can influence events through participating in Commons committees and voting in debates. Although the strength of their influence depends on the size of the government's overall majority and the unity of the government, Opposition MPs are, as the title suggests, in opposition. They do not create events, but respond to them.

Next in the power stakes are government MPs. Most 'backbench' government ment MPs would like promotion in their parliamentary career, so they are likely to be loyal to the Executive. They also, presumably, support the main thrust of the Executive's Commons programme, so they are likely to obey the Whips over most legislation. At the very least, if the Executive loses popularity they are likely to lose popularity too, and lose their job at the next election. So, most of the time, backbench MPs have a vested interest in supporting Executive legislation. This is why they are sometimes referred to as 'lobby fodder'. Rebellions do happen though, as we shall see.

At the centre of power is the Executive itself. The Executive is composed of 'frontbench' MPs. These promoted MPs are usually known as Ministers. The Prime Minister (as the title suggests) is the most powerful of them all. He/she is known as 'first among equals'.

This is the context in which all debates on Parliament/Executive power lies.

The balance of power varies from one government to the next. Crucially, the balance of power within the Executive varies from one Prime Minister to the next. There are a wide variety of constitutional powers any Prime Minister can use.

Tony Blair, for example, has been a quite remarkable Prime Minister. It has become very apparent that he is a strong leader who is prepared to use his constitutional and personal powers to stamp his authority on the Cabinet and Parliament. This is not new. Margaret

Thatcher had an 'inner Cabinet' of specially trusted colleagues with whom she consulted. Cabinet meetings were short and businesslike, rather than opportunities for collective debate. Tony Blair has, in fact, bypassed Cabinet many times in his decision making, relying on the advice of outside 'political advisers' and 'think tanks' to form policy.

THE PRIME MINISTER AND PARLIAMENT

Tony Blair has had every opportunity to be a very powerful Prime Minister. He, unlike John Major before him, has had two huge parliamentary majorities. After the May 2005 general election his majority was reduced to 67, and it is interesting to observe how much less powerful he has been with this reduced 'mandate' from the public.

Since 2005, Tony Blair has had to negotiate with his Cabinet and parliamentary colleagues much more on issues ranging from reform of public services, such as health and education, to anti-terrorism and identity cards.

Prior to 2005, Labour Party Whips had an easy time managing MPs' voting behaviour. Blair's reforms of the Labour Party and the dominance of Blairite ideas both within the Cabinet and among Labour backbenchers, meant there was little support for rebellion within the Party.

The war in Iraq saw the first real crisis for the Prime
Minister's power. The late Robin Cook resigned as Foreign Secretary, and Clare Short ultimately resigned as Secretary of State for International Development.
Nevertheless, there was no widespread revolt within the Labour Party. The opposition parties were unable to land a knockout blow. Why was this the case?

Former Prime Minister, Harold Macmillan, once said when asked what he feared most,
"Events, dear boy, events."

External events are critical. The continued success of the British economy—low inflation, low unemployment and low interest rates—kept Tony Blair in command. Bad economic news combined with unpopular international issues can lead to parliamentary rebellions which no Prime Minister can live with.

The unpopularity of the poll tax, combined with deepening economic problems, brought the downfall of Margaret Thatcher, the 'iron lady'. It takes more than talented, hard-working MPs to successfully oppose the Executive.

The Conservatives and the other opposition parties know this. So long as the government maintains economic stability, its chances of defeat in Commons votes are low.

Tony Blair knows this too, which is why his energies have been spent elsewhere than in the Commons.
Tony Blair has, by comparison with other Prime Ministers and party leaders, had little time for debates in the House of Commons. *The Times* newspaper reported that in the 2003–04 parliamentary session, Tony Blair attended only 6% of Commons votes. His average of 8% since 1997 is well
below that of his predecessors, John Major and Margaret Thatcher.

Control of the Cabinet Agenda

The Prime Minister has the power to control the Cabinet. As 'first among equals' the PM decides when the Cabinet will meet, how long the meeting will take and what will be discussed.

The evidence so far from Tony Blair's premiership is that he has by-passed the Cabinet in a lot of decisions. According to the political journalist James Naughtie,

"no Prime Minister since the nineteenth century has spent more time avoiding formal meetings with Cabinet colleagues than Tony Blair".

The real deals are done elsewhere, usually in the Prime Minister's study, with three or four of Tony Blair's key allies (Alasdair Campbell, Jonathan Powell, Anji Hunter) present.

Blair's Cabinet meetings are very short, an hour at most, with some lasting only thirty minutes. Former Cabinet colleagues have said that Cabinet meetings are a conversation between two people—Tony Blair and Gordon Brown—no one else is taken seriously. Brown looks after domestic social and economic policy, while Blair sees to foreign issues and certain favourite topics in domestic policy, such as health and Northern Ireland.

Tony Blair's Cabinet barely discussed crucial issues such as the war in Iraq in any great detail. Decisions were made outside the Cabinet by Blair and his advisers.

Blair seems to have moved not just the Commons, but also the Cabinet, to the very edge of decision making. His conduct strengthens the case of those who claim we now have a British President rather than a Prime Minister.

Parliament as an arena for conflict

Prime Minister's Question Time is the Prime Minister's opportunity to show his command of the issues which face the country. Tony Blair has been an exceptional performer at Question Time. He is well briefed by his army of senior civil servants and political advisers, so only very rarely is he caught out by awkward questions from the opposition parties.

For most of Tony Blair's Premiership, the Labour Party was popular in the polls and he enjoyed command of both his party and the Commons. In addition to having large parliamentary majorities, he was also helped by the long-term divisions within the Conservative Party and its continual search for a winning leader.

In recent times, Tony Blair has been faced with a reinvigorated Conservative Opposition under the leadership of David Cameron. Cameron has, to date, been a competent adversary for Tony Blair at Question Time and the exchanges have enhanced Cameron's status as a possible future Prime Minister.

Given that Tony Blair will not run again for Prime Minister, Cameron can only benefit from gaining experience at Question Time before the new Labour leader can find his/her feet.

Blair v Brown

Gordon Brown has become the longest serving, and some would say most successful, Chancellor in British political history. Most politicians stay as Chancellor for about three years before being reshuffled, but Gordon Brown has never been asked to move.

Tony Blair knows that Gordon Brown has a great deal of support in the Labour Party and that sacking Brown would have led to rebellion within the Party. Blair has been very clever to keep Brown as part of his team, muzzled by the concept of 'collective responsibility'. Collective responsibility means that once decisions are made in Cabinet, and minutes of Cabinet meetings are often not released for thirty years, all Cabinet Ministers must support the decision taken, regardless of their personal opinions.

Gordon Brown, as his supporters have let it be known, has been unhappy with Tony Blair's leadership, but so long as he is in the Cabinet he dare not speak out too much.

Tony Blair's Black Wednesday

In November 2005, after eight years in power, Tony Blair's government suffered its first ever Commons defeat on the issue of detaining terrorist suspects. Labour rebels, who had not forgiven Blair for the war in Iraq, tasted blood. Tony Blair also lost the House of Commons Education vote in March 2006. Blair himself admitted it was a 'high wire act'. As Harold Macmillan commented fifty years previously, a combination of events conspired to take power away from the Prime Minister.

Tony Blair may have felt that the Commons votes on terrorism and education were traumatic, but they were nothing compared to Labour's 'Black Wednesday' of 26 April 2006.

The original 'Black Wednesday' happened to John Major's Conservatives in 1992. Despite promising that the pound would not be devalued and despite spending millions of pounds maintaining its value, Chancellor Norman Lamont (pictured above) was forced to devalue the currency to keep Britain in the European Exchange Rate Mechanism. The government was clearly not in control of the economy. The Chancellor resigned and the Conservatives never led in the polls again. They have been out of power since 1997. Once this indefinable 'trust' in a government is lost it is very hard to win back.

On Labour's 'Black Wednesday':

- Deputy Prime Minister John Prescott was found to have been having an affair with a party researcher. This was not illegal, but it was embarrassing.

- Much worse was the calamity at the Home Office. Numerous criminals who were born outwith the UK who should have been deported on release from prison had been set free.

- On top of all this, nurses booed the Health Minister, Patricia Hewitt, over NHS reforms and the government was accused of accepting loans to the Labour Party in return for political honours.

It all began to look as if the government, especially Tony Blair, had lost course. It was reminiscent of the worst days of 'Tory sleaze' in the mid-90s, the kind of issue Tony Blair and John Prescott had campaigned against so vigorously and successfully.

Voters in England and Wales passed judgement on the government's performance in the May 2006 local government elections. Hundreds of Labour councillors, who had nothing to do with the above events, lost their jobs.

The Conservatives, under new leader David Cameron (opposite), got their best election results since 1992. In the opinion polls, Tony Blair's personal approval ratings of 26% were even lower than Harold Wilson's in 1968 when he devalued the pound.

A number of Labour MPs, a far wider group than the 'usual suspects' of anti-Blair left-wingers, signed a letter to the PM asking him for a 'timetable' of when he would resign. His successor-in-waiting, Gordon Brown, spoke in coded language of this being the time for the government to "renew itself".

The Prime Minister's power had been weakened against both Cabinet rivals and parliamentary opponents. In spite of all this, the Prime Minister remained in charge.

PRIME MINISTERIAL POWER IN ACTION

The Prime Minster has the crucial the power of patronage. S/He can appoint MPs to the Cabinet and also remove them. S/He can award peerages in the Lords or political honours. This creates loyalty and obedience among the MPs in his/her party.

The Prime Minister will always pick a Cabinet team s/he knows to be 'on-message'. Blair packed his Cabinets with his most trusted allies and froze out the mavericks and those who were not 'modernisers'.

The Prime Minister's response to 'Black Wednesday' was classic Blair. He saw this setback as an opportunity to push on with New Labour, rather than compromise with his opponents. In a decisive Cabinet reshuffle, Blair dropped John Prescott from his job as Leader of the House of Commons, but controversially allowed him to keep his ministerial house and car.

Treat your friends better than you treat your enemies is a classic rule of power and one which Blair chose to follow. The Prime Minister then rewarded other 'Blairites' with key jobs. John Reid was moved from Defence to the Home Office to sort out Charles Clarke's mess. Margaret Beckett, who has been loyal to New Labour, was given the job of Foreign Secretary. Douglas Alexander was moved to the combined job of Transport and Scottish Secretary and Des Browne was given John Reid's old job of Defence Secretary.

Key issue:
To what extent can pressure groups influence the decision making process?

Some pressure groups, depending on the circumstances, have more influence than others. For example, the Confederation of British Industry (CBI) is an 'insider' pressure group for the Labour government. The Prime Minister is very keen to have the support of business. He will seek out the views of leading business people. If the CBI says that it does not want interest rates to rise, the government will listen carefully. The CBI and also the British Medical Association (BMA), which represents the country's doctors, are therefore on the 'inside track' of government. As such, they are often described as 'insider groups'.

On the other hand, groups such as the often controversial 'Fathers 4 Justice', are very much 'outsider groups'. Tony Blair will not seek out their views and they are highly unlikely to change his mind.

Insider Groups

Insider groups pursue very different methods from outsider groups to achieve their goals. They do not need to have marches or demonstrations. Instead they will have regular meetings with government, either at local government, Scottish Executive or Westminster level.

Relationships between the government and insider pressure groups will be professional and constructive. They may not always agree and neither side will necessarily get all it wants, but there is likely to be long lasting communication between the two. Sometimes insider groups are elevated by the government to the position of 'stakeholder'. This occurs when the insider group is seen as a 'partner', rather than a nuisance.

The BMA is an insider group

Some pressure groups, such as the British Medical Association which have a lot of specialist, professional expertise (and public support) are viewed by the government as stakeholders. For example, if the government was planning to reform the health system, it could be harmful if the BMA was against its plans. The BMA is well organised and has a lot of public support. The public is likely to support local health experts, rather than the government, on a chosen issue. This was shown when the Labour Party which had been in power since 1997, lost the Kidderminster seat to a local GP in the 2001 general election.

The strength of the government's majority in the House of Commons and the state of the opposition are big factors affecting the influence of pressure groups. Up until now, Tony Blair's government has had a big Commons majority and the Conservatives have been very divided.

This meant that the government was confident of winning the next election and individual MPs were confident of retaining their seats. Both the government and individual Labour MPs, therefore, were not as vulnerable from the activities of pressure groups.

Outsider Groups

However, in circumstances where the government has a smaller Commons majority, pressure groups may feel that they have an opportunity to exert more power on a weakened Executive.

Pressure groups need to be strategic about who they seek to apply pressure to. There is no point 'lobbying' Westminster if it is a devolved or local issue the group is concerned about. Increasingly, the Scottish Parliament is becoming the focus for pressure group lobby-ing as groups realise that their issue is a devolved one, rather than an issue reserved to Westminster.

Not all outsider groups are the same. There are degrees of being an outsider group. It is fair to say that a terrorist group such as al-Qaeda is right on the margins.

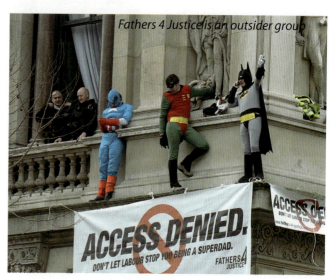

Fathers 4 Justice is an outsider group

Groups such as Fathers 4 Justice, who use attention seeking stunts, can also be described as outsider groups. It is because they are on the outside that they take extreme measures to capture public attention. However, others are not so far out. Scotland's 'Cool Crusaders' have organised a petition to try to change European Union quotas on North Sea fishing. They have the support of respected politicians such as the SNP leader, Alex Salmond.

Some pressure groups go through phases of being outside then inside, depending on the political complexion of the government. In the 1970s trade unions, in the form of the Trades Union Congress (TUC), were powerful and their views were listened to. Under an 'old' Labour government, trade unions were very much on the inside track.

However, the Conservative governments of the 1980s put the trade unions back outside. New Labour has kept the trade unions at arms length. Trade unions are not as frozen out as they were in the Conservative days, but neither are they given the 'special status' they would like from a Labour government. The trade unions have been most upset that the Blair Labour government has preferred to listen to the views of their traditional opponents, the CBI.

The Make Poverty History campaign is an interesting example of a pressure group which is both inside and outside the decision making process. Make Poverty History is an umbrella group in the sense that there are many different pressure groups operating under that banner. In the run-up to the G8 Summit at Gleneagles in 2005, some pressure groups, such as Scottish Catholic International Aid Fund (SCIAF) were clearly on the inside, presenting papers to the summit and gaining the ear of top decision makers, such as Chancellor Gordon Brown. Others, though,

were obviously outside. Anti-globalisation protesters sought to disrupt the meeting and put a wholly different kind of pressure on the G8.

Ultimately, it is very difficult to evaluate the impact which pressure groups make on the decision making process.

The influence of insider groups is likely to be unspectacular and long term. The things they do will not make banner headlines in newspapers. '**DOCTORS MEET WITH SCOTTISH EXECUTIVE**' would not sell too many newspapers.

Even when outsider pressure groups have a great deal of media coverage and popular support, it is difficult to evaluate how successful they are. Hundreds of thousands of people protested over poverty in Africa. The Make Poverty History campaign put African poverty on the front page of every newspaper. The issue was discussed at the G8 summit and without the Make Poverty History activities, it may never have been raised at all. But has it made any difference? Make Poverty History protesters disagree among themselves over how much difference they have made.

Perhaps it is better to ask what would happen if pressure groups, both insider and outsider, did not get involved in the political process? How would the poor and the marginalised make their predicament known? Hundreds of thousands of people marched against the war in Iraq, but the war went ahead anyway. However, the campaign against the war has damaged Tony Blair. Many Labour MPs lost their seats in the 2005 general election. How much has the Labour government been damaged by all the negative publicity surrounding the war in Iraq?

We live in a democracy where, if the issue is popular enough, the government must listen and respond in some way, or it will lose at the ballot box.

Key issue:
To what extent do civil servants influence decision making?

THE CIVIL SERVICE

Most people's view of civil servants is coloured by the BBC series Yes Minister. The theme of the series is the way in which devious civil servants manipulate government ministers. Ministers are, after all, here today, gone tomorrow. Civil servants work much longer in government departments.

Government ministers have many different demands on their time and energies. They therefore place great trust in their team of civil servants to provide them with reliable information. Civil servants, based in the one department for a length of time, develop considerable expertise in the areas in which they work. According to the Yes Minister model, civil servants do not trust Ministers. Ministers, according to this theory, work to a different agenda. They need to be re-elected and so they need policies which will bring short-term popularity. Civil servants, on the other hand, are always there.

In the Yes Minister programme, the fiendish Sir Humphrey hoodwinks the Minister, including the Prime Minister, into agreeing to policy options which the civil service favours. All of this, if true, would be highly undemocratic. Ministers, wise or foolish, are elected by the people. Senior civil servants are appointed, not elected.

The most senior civil servants traditionally come from social classes A and B. It is claimed by their critics that they have an inbuilt bias in favour of 'conservative' solutions.

As with all stereotypes, there may be a basis of truth somewhere, but the Yes Minister view of the civil service does not do justice to the complexity of relations which goes on in government. There may well be bumbling, easily duped Ministers and there may well be devious civil servants, but in the vast majority of cases, both Ministers and civil servants work together with common goals. The relationship is one of 'mutual dependency'.

Although relationships between civil servants and Ministers may be changing fast relations between civil servants and the public are changing faster.

The Civil Service Code

The civil service is officially known as the Home Civil Service. Civil servants have to work within strict rules, known as the Civil Service Code. The Civil Service Code sets out the constitutional framework within which all civil servants must work and the values they are expected to uphold.

The constitutional and practical role of the civil service is to assist the UK government at Westminster, the Scottish Executive at Holyrood, the National Assembly for Wales in Cardiff or the Northern Ireland Assembly at Stormont with integrity, honesty, impartiality and objectivity. Civil servants are servants of the Crown. Scottish Executive civil servants are accountable to Scottish Ministers, who are themselves accountable to the Scottish Parliament.

The civil service in Scotland remains part of the Home Civil Service. However, civil servants working for the Scottish Executive owe their loyalty to the devolved administration rather than to the UK government. The Scottish Executive is the devolved government for Scotland. It is responsible for most of the issues of day-to-day concern to the people of Scotland, including health, education, justice, rural affairs, and transport. In the financial year 2005–2006 it managed an annual budget of more than £27 billion, which is due to rise to over £30 billion in 2007–2008.

The Scottish Executive was established in 1999, following the first elections to the Scottish Parliament. It is currently a coalition between the Scottish Labour Party and the Scottish Liberal Democrat Party. The Scottish Executive is led by the First Minister, who is elected by the Parliament. He/she has the power of appointing the other Scottish Ministers who make up the Cabinet.

There are increasing drives to achieve 'best value' in government. Civil servants are trained to deal with the public efficiently, promptly and without bias. Civil service departments have rules which compel them to ensure 'best value' i.e. the most effective and efficient use of public money.

Civil servants should not misuse their official position or any information acquired in the course of their official duties to further their private interests or those of others. They should not receive benefits of any kind from a third party which might reasonably be seen to compromise their personal judgement or integrity.

Relations between Ministers and civil servants

The job of, for example, the Scottish Education Minister, is to implement the education policies of the Scottish Executive. A good Minister will have a vision of where he/she wants Scottish education to go. He/she may have arrived from a non-education background. Nevertheless, he/she will make an effort to 'get on top of the brief' by speaking to trusted colleagues, practitioners on the ground, 'insider' pressure groups, and, in this case, teachers, pupils and parents. He/she will, of course, also rely on the advice and expertise of the civil servants in the Scottish Education Department.

The role of the civil service is to advise the Minister on how best to implement those policies s/he and the wider Scottish Executive have decided upon. It is not the civil servant's job to make up or decide on those policies, but to offer advice on their successful implementation.

In reality, the relationship becomes one of mutual dependence. The Minister is surrounded by many experts within the Civil Service. In time, s/he will know which civil servants s/he can trust to provide her/him with expert, accurate, up-to-date information.

In turn, civil servants want to see 'their' Minister succeed. There is a professional pride in seeing policies succeeding and life for the public improving. Civil servants receive promotion based on performance. The ability to support Ministers with high quality advice and information is the key to promotion.

A civil servant who can display expertise in the qualities of the Civil Service Code is a civil servant on the way to the top. A civil servant who was disloyal to a Minister or to other colleagues in the departmental team would not receive promotion and could in fact be disciplined.

When a Minister speaks in the House of Commons, civil servants will prepare her/him for the debate. They will draft her/his speech. They will make the Minister aware of likely 'points of attack' by the Opposition and arm her/him with facts and figures to rebut their case.

In the case of media management, a vital aspect of modern politics, civil servants will prepare news releases for television, press and radio. They will 'spin' information in such a way as to project the best possible image of the Minister's work and direct attention to areas in which the Minister has made the most progress.

Civil servants who support the First Minister in the Scottish Parliament or the Prime Minister in the House of Commons have an even trickier job. One of the main responsibilities of the Prime Minister is to answer questions put to her/him at Question Time. The main question from Opposition MPs is usually tame, but the 'supplementary' questions are the tricky ones and could be on any aspect of government policy. It could be about the war on terror, but it could also be about drugs policy, nuclear power, housing, or any number of issues. It is the job of the Prime Minister's team of civil servants and special advisers to guess correctly what the supplementary questions will be in order to ensure that the Prime Minister can answer them well to avoid political defeat.

In fact the image of Sir Humphrey in Yes Minister is quite wide of the mark. The relationship between Minister and civil servant is rarely exploitative, but is normally symbiotic (one supporting the other). A Minister with drive and competence will motivate civil servants to work better and more efficiently. A Minister with a talented civil service team behind her/him will be a better politician.

By contrast, opposition politicians do not have the support of the machinery of government. They must prepare for parliamentary debates, such as Question Time, with only the support of party researchers. While frequently very talented, researchers are often young and inexperienced. The Opposition is disadvantaged through lacking the high quality resources the government can call upon.

Ministers have the whole of Parliament's agencies, researchers and advisers, and thousands of salaried staff to arm them with information.

Criticism from both the political Left and political Right

From the Left, socialists view senior civil servants as, at best, conservative with a small 'c', and, at worst, Conservative with a capital 'C'. They believe that their backgrounds, normally from the elite schools and universities, take them away from the concerns of 'normal' people.

It is claimed their bias may be calculated (e.g. against policies which help 'undeserving' poorer people) but more often critics claim the bias is likely to be unconscious. Because senior civil servants' personal lives and social contacts are so divorced from the lives of the socially excluded, their advice is influenced by 'middle-class' attitudes and expectations.

The Right distrusts the civil service too. They feel that the civil service is unwilling to consider private sector solutions. Furthermore, they claim that because the civil service is a government body, it has a vested interest in raising taxes and spending money in the public sector to preserve the jobs and careers of its members.

The Right believes the civil service is inefficient and undynamic. It would like to see more people from business and the private sector brought in to give advice to Ministers.

Special Advisers

Special Advisers are employed to help Ministers on matters where the work of government and the work of the government party overlap and it would be inappro-

priate for permanent civil servants to become involved. They are an additional source for the Minister providing advice from a standpoint that is more politically committed and politically aware than would be available to a Minister from the civil service.

Special Advisers are often described as 'spin doctors'. A large part of their job is to 'spin' information so that it is presented to the media and the public in such a way as to show the government in the most positive light possible.

Special Advisers are temporary civil servants appointed under Article 3 of the civil service Order. They are exempt from the general requirement that civil servants should be appointed on merit and behave with political impartiality and objectivity so that they may retain the confidence of future governments of a different political complexion.

There is a strong overlap between their government work and their party political work. Only a very loyal party member, one who is completely 'on-message' with the government, will be employed as a Special Adviser.

In Scotland, there is a limit of twelve Special Advisers allowed in any one administration. At Westminster, advisers such as Alastair Campbell and Jonathan Powell have had great influence. Special Advisers in Scotland are not allowed managerial control over civil servants.

The total cost to the Scottish taxpayer of Special Advisers is now around £750,000 per year. Opposition critics claim this money is used to promote the interests of the governing parties rather than the interests of the country as a whole.

A Special Adviser's appointment ends at the end of the administration which appointed her/him. The responsibility for the management and conduct of Special Advisers, including discipline, rests with the Minister who made the appointment.

Jo Moore is perhaps the most infamous Special Adviser. As Special Adviser to the Transport Secretary in 2001, Stephen Byers, Jo Moore sent an email stating that 11 September 2001, the day of the al-Qaeda attacks on the USA, was "a very good day to get out anything we want to bury". Jo Moore's message was timed at 14.55 BST on 11 September, within an hour of the second plane flying into the World Trade Center, but before either tower collapsed. Jo Moore was forced to resign after widespread condemnation of her actions.

Study Theme 1D
Electoral Systems, Voting and Political Attitudes

Reference to the Pulse Publications textbook, *UK Politics Today*, Chapters 1 and 2 and www.modernityscotland.com will enhance the use of these revision notes. It is assumed that you have studied the course and have a sound understanding of the key political issues in the UK.

EXAM REQUIREMENTS

You are expected to display knowledge and understanding of:

1   The UK, Scottish, European Parliamentary and Scottish local government electoral systems; the effects of these systems on the distribution of power within and among parties, in elected bodies and between the electorate and the elected.

2   Voting patterns; explanations of voting behaviour.

3   The shaping of political attitudes through the media; opinion polls; referenda; voter participation.

Key issue:
How fair are different voting systems and what are the advantages and disadvantages of each?

The introduction of proportional representation (PR) is not an abstract debate. It is not a case of do we keep the first-past-the-post voting system or do we bring in a system of PR? PR is here already! At the moment in the UK, we are using four different kinds of voting system, three of which are based on a system of PR.

System 1	First-past-the-post *UK Parliament general election*
System 2	The Additional Member System (AMS) *Scottish Parliament elections*
System 3	The Single Transferable Vote (STV) *Northern Ireland* *Scottish local government elections from 2007*
System 4	Party List system *European Parliament elections*

We will review the first three systems in this chapter.

ADVANTAGES OF FIRST-PAST-THE-POST

FPTP usually produces a decisive result

The key word here is usually. The last seven general elections have produced a decisive result with one party winning enough seats in the House of Commons to form a government with an overall majority.

At an FPTP election, the voters have a choice of parties wishing to be in government. The parties present their manifestos to the voters. These contain the pledges which would be made into law should they win power. The governing party has up to five years to deliver its manifesto promises. If it does not manage this, it has no one else to blame—it had the majority in the House of Commons to pass any laws it wished.

At the end of those five years, the voters judge whether it was a success or not. At the 2005 election, Labour was elected with only 36% of the overall vote. Is it better to please some of the people than have coalitions which could, after all, please none of the people?

FPTP usually delivers stable government

Here in the UK, we are used to stable government. By this we mean general elections or major changes in government are few and far between. It may be dull, but it is good for the economy and our quality of life. Business, especially global business, does not like instability. It likes to know what interest rates, currency rates, inflation rates and government policies will be over the long term. Governments which change frequently are bad news for the economy. For this reason it is argued that stable government, even if the result is slightly unfair, is better than the instability that PR systems allegedly can bring.

FPTP allows voters to protest

There are usually by-elections in an FPTP voting system. These happen when an MP retires or dies. These can be used by the voters to show their disapproval of a government which has gone off course. For example in the Dunfermline West by-election of February 2006 the Liberal Democrat candidate, Willie Rennie, won a 'safe' Labour seat. Voters in Dunfermline West took the opportunity to protest against the governing Labour Party.

DISADVANTAGES OF FIRST-PAST-THE-POST

Hung parliaments happen under FPTP

FPTP does not always produce decisive results. In 1977–79, Labour had to go into coalition with the Liberal Party. In 1996–97, John Major's Conservatives went into coalition with the Ulster Unionists. Was it democratic that the Ulster Unionists (who only represent constituencies in Northern Ireland) should run the country?

Do we get a fair result?

The 2005 general election was described by *The Independent* newspaper as the most unfair election result of all time. Because of FPTP, Labour was allowed to run the country on its own for five years on the basis of achieving 35.2% of the votes cast. The Liberal Democrats won 22% of the votes but gained only 10% of the seats.

Is strong government good government?

Stability is good, but is strong government always good government? Is it not better to have another point of view in the government to produce better government? There is an argument that says the longer a party is in power on its own, the more likely it is to produce policies the voters do not like.

Margaret Thatcher's Conservatives came up with the Poll Tax, a policy so unpopular that it led to fighting in the streets and her eventual downfall as Prime Minister. Likewise, if Labour had been in a coalition government, rather than having outright power, would we have had the war in Iraq?

Try to avoid weak arguments which do not really stand up to much analysis. Four examples of such arguments are given below.

"FPTP produces majority governments."
As we have seen this does not always happen. In March 2006, Tony Blair needed the votes of Conservative MPs to have his Education Bill passed in the House of Commons. So much for FPTP producing a decisive result.

"The two big parties do well under FPTP."
Labour does do well but the Tories do not. At the last general election, the Tories did almost as well as Labour, winning 32.3% of the vote, but they gained far fewer seats. This is because of the current boundary arrangements.
Labour constituencies tend to be smaller and have smaller majorities. The Conservatives are more likely to win bigger constituencies with bigger majorities. It is harder therefore for the Conservatives to translate their votes into seats.
For the Conservatives to win the next election, they will probably need to have a 7% lead over Labour nationally to overcome the demographic advantage the current FPTP system gives Labour.

"The Liberal Democrats do not do well under FPTP"
In one sense they do not, but the Liberal Democrats are becoming increasingly aware of how to use FPTP to their advantage. The Liberal Democrats lie in second place in most seats in England. By clever use of tactical voting, the Liberal Democrats could, in theory, keep the Conservatives, especially, out of power for a generation.

"FPTP creates a link between voter and MP."
Can you name your local MP? Do you know where he/she holds his/her surgeries? Have you ever contacted your MP? Do you know how he/she voted on any Bill in the House of Commons? Outwith election time, few voters have any meaningful link with their MP. Voters, except in exceptional circumstances, vote for parties, not individuals.

Why bother voting?

Because FPTP is based on winning 646 individual constituencies, parties with a strong social class base in these constituencies have an advantage. For example, most constituencies in Glasgow are in working-class areas where Labour is strongest. Why should a Conservative voter in, for example Govan, bother to vote? Realistically, his/her vote is likely to be of no consequence at all.

ADVANTAGES OF AMS

Gives smaller parties a chance

Not all voters in Scotland support the established parties. Because of the Additional Member System (AMS), the supporters of the Scottish Socialists, Solidarity, the Green Party and the Scottish Senior Citizens Unity Party can have their say in how the country is run.

It is unlikely that any one party will have complete control

AMS usually leads to coalition government and in the elections so far to the Scottish Parliament this has happened. This, it is argued, is a good thing. For example, the compromise over tuition fees, with the repayment of fees postponed until after the student has gained a job with a professional salary, is seen as an honourable and sensible policy made after compromise and negotiation between two partners in government.

Every vote counts

In the AMS, every vote is recycled and reallocated, giving every voter in every constituency an incentive to vote. There is no such thing as a 'wasted vote'.

AMS increases the number of excluded groups in parliament

Since parties need not disclose the names of their list candidates, it is argued that they can move away from having the same white, male candidates and have a broader selection of representatives in parliament. The SNP has placed Bashir Ahmed, who is an Asian, in a prominent place in its rankings for list members of the Scottish Parliament following the election in 2007

Again, avoid weak arguments which do not really stand up to much analysis. Three example are:

"The AMS is complicated."
The insides of cars are complicated, but that does not stop people driving them. Likewise with AMS the calculations are complicated, and you can study these all day and night if you really want to, but voting itself is very easy. What is so complicated about voting twice rather than just once?

"It takes ages to work out the results."
It maybe takes about a couple of hours longer than FPTP. Is it not better to take your time and get the fairest result, rather than the quickest?

"It leads to unstable coalitions."
Scotland, so far, has had two different coalitions (or 'partnerships') since 1999. There have been tensions. Labour and the Liberal Democrats are different parties and are political rivals, but they have worked together. The Scottish Executive has been very stable.

DISADVANTAGES OF AMS

Unelected MSPs

Who is Andrew Arbuckle MSP? He is a Liberal Democrat List MSP for mid-Scotland and Fife, but who voted for him? He is an MSP because Keith Raffan MSP, the previous Liberal Democrat MSP for mid-Scotland and Fife, resigned due to 'stress'. The Liberal Democrat party members voted to replace Keith Raffan with Andrew Arbuckle. However, no member of the public had a say in who their MSP should be. Is this fair?

MSP turf wars?

Who is the 'real' MSP for your area? Is it the constituency MSP, or is it one of your other seven list MSPs? Which one should you turn to? Who should get the credit for improving your area? If life in your area is not so good, are you 'blaming' the right person or is it nothing to do with them?

There is no doubt there is rivalry between the two 'classes' of MSP in the Scottish Parliament. The constituency MSPs think of themselves as 'real' MSPs and sometimes resent the 'encroachment' of list MSPs on 'their turf'.

Parties become more powerful than voters

In some parties, the place on the party list is more important than connecting with voters. Most of the Conservative and SNP MSPs are list MSPs. To become an MSP for one these parties, it is more important to appeal to small groups of party activists than it is to communicate with the wider voters. First or second place on the Conservative or Scottish National Party list will mean you have a good chance of being elected to the Scottish Parliament. The voter need never even know your name.

A government no one voted for

At least under FPTP, you have a straightforward choice. Your party may not win the election, but at least you know what you are going to get from the party who does.

In an AMS coalition, you can have a 'partnership' that was never presented on any ballot paper and policies that no one had the chance to vote for. For example, the Liberal Democrats finished fourth in the last Scottish Parliament election. Is it fair that they should be running the country with Labour? Who voted for this?

ADVANTAGES OF STV

STV allows the voter to choose within parties

The added value of STV is that it allows voters to choose within as well as between parties. For example, you may be a Labour voter but dislike the Labour candidate. Under STV you can cast your vote for the Labour candidate you like, ignoring the one you dislike. Alternatively, you could like a Conservative candidate, but not the Conservative Party. You can now vote for this candidate but not the others the Conservatives put forward.

All votes count

Just like the AMS, all votes are tallied up and reallocated. There are no wasted votes. Incidentally, a voter does not have to use all the votes he/she has. He/she can rank in order of preference, but if there is only one candidate he/she wishes to vote for he/she simply writes in '1' beside that name and walks away.

STV gives smaller parties a greater chance

Like the AMS, the STV gives smaller parties a better chance of being elected. This is why Labour councillors in our big cities are so opposed to STV. They know FPTP suits them and many are likely to lose their seats in 2007.

STV empowers voters, not political parties

A disadvantage of the AMS is that closed lists (where parties need not declare their candidates' names) happen. Under STV, this does not happen. Voters therefore have more choice in picking both people and parties.

DISADVANTAGES OF STV

It is harder for smaller parties than AMS

The AMS has a smaller threshold than STV. This means that it usually only takes about 4% of votes to elect an MSP under the list system, but it will probably take about 7% of votes to elect a representative under STV. Therefore, in terms of helping smaller parties, the AMS is better than STV.

Multi-members confuse voters

Under STV there are bigger constituencies, which in the case of rural, Highland Scotland may not be a good thing, with the obvious difficulties of transport. There is also the same problem which the AMS has with 'where does the buck stop'? Who is the representative who is responsible for decisions taken at a local level? Voters have more than one local representative and each could blame the other for not getting things done.

STV could create unrepresentative 'kingmakers'

Just like the AMS, we can have a situation where one party, e.g. the Liberal Democrats, could have power disproportionate to their support in the country.

The following three arguments about STV are weak and should be avoided.

"It is is too complicated."
The analogy of the car holds for STV too. All the voters need to do is rank the candidates and/or their parties 1, 2, 3 etc. Surely that is not too difficult? Yes, the sums are complicated, but computers can work these sums out, the voters need not worry or care.

"The link between MP and voter is removed."
If anything, the link between representative and voter is strengthened under STV. An MP can no longer think, "I'm the Labour candidate, I'll get elected next time." S/He probably will not be the only Labour candidate, so surely representatives under STV need to work harder to have a link with voters?

"Leads to unstable coalitions."
The Scottish Parliament Information Centre (SPICe) carried out research into the Republic of Ireland's STV system. It concluded:

> "On the whole there has been no excessive frequency either of elections or of changes of government in the Republic of Ireland."

In other words, in the Republic of Ireland's case, STV has not led to unstable coalitions.

EXPLANATIONS OF VOTING BEHAVIOUR

The Influence of Social Class

The classic definition of the influence of social class on voting behaviour comes from the sociologists, Butler and Stokes. Their 1970 work on social class famously concluded that social class was the major issue affecting voting behaviour. Everything else was "embellishment and detail". However, 1970 was a long time ago. Does social class still have this major influence or have other issues become more important?

Up until the 1970s there was a clear two-party system in UK elections. Labour was seen to be the champion of the 'working class', while the Conservatives were perceived to support the interests of the 'middle' and 'upper classes'. Elections were won (more often than not by the Conservatives) on who could win over 'floating' middle-class voters.

The process of social class 'dealignment' began in the 1970s and has continued to this day. Dealignment means that voters no longer believe themselves to be committed supporters of a political party on the basis of their social class.

According to political scientist Ivor Crewe, a new working class has emerged: the so-called C1 and C2 classes. Sometimes referred to as 'Mondeo Man', this key group of skilled workers rejected Labour's traditional collectivist approach, favouring Margaret Thatcher's Conservative, individualist path to prosperity,

The last general election in 2005 saw social class remaining a key influence. For example, the higher up the social class ladder we look, the greater the turnout of voters. The lower down the class ladder we look, the fewer people we see voting.

Social class remains a major influence on voting behaviour, but social class is quite a complex issue these days. Unlike in the 1970s, it is not so easy to define who exactly is 'working' or 'middle' class. There is, of course, the official National Statistics definition of social class. By this definition, the middle class has grown.

Classes D and E could, perhaps, safely be termed 'working class'. But what of C1 and C2? These are skilled workers, for example NHS nurses who do responsible jobs which require many educational qualifications. Are nurses middle or working class?

Many working-class families now own their own homes. Home ownership used to be a standard definition of middle-class status. Many more people now have degrees and professional occupations. Likewise,

many people who in some respects may see themselves as working class, may have incomes, assets and lifestyles which could put them in the middle-class bracket.

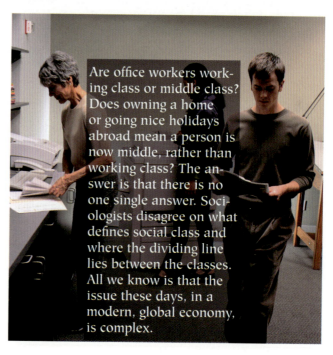

Are office workers working class or middle class? Does owning a home or going nice holidays abroad mean a person is now middle, rather than working class? The answer is that there is no one single answer. Sociologists disagree on what defines social class and where the dividing line lies between the classes. All we know is that the issue these days, in a modern, global economy, is complex.

The political parties, of course, realise this.

As a result, the parties are now 'catch all parties', who seek to present policies which will attract a 'big tent' of voters across the social classes. Labour's welfare to work policies are typical 'big tent' policies.

Getting people off benefits into work through, for example, the National Minimum Wage, appeals to Labour's 'core' working-class voters. However, welfare to work, for instance, the New Deals, will appeal to high income voters who may resent their taxes being 'squandered' on welfare benefits. The New Deal gets people off benefits into work. Thus welfare to work creates a 'big tent' of voters—core Labour voters like it, but 'floating' voters like it too.

Putting yourself in the picture with New Deal 50 plus

new deal*

Social Class Core Voters

All the major political parties have their 'core voters'. Core voters are ideologically driven, even if they do not necessarily realise this. Core Labour voters, for example, feel Labour is 'their' party, 'for people like them'. Core voters rarely discuss party policies. Their minds are made up. The only danger for the political parties is apathy. They must make sure their core voters actually vote.

Labour won the 2005 general election with a much reduced majority. In most cases this was not because Labour voters switched to other parties. It was because they chose not to vote at all for various reasons.

Labour knows its core voters are working class and that they live, and vote, in specific Labour 'heartlands'. These, invariably, are constituencies with large urban areas, especially those with high numbers of council houses.

Labour's core voters are working class

Core Labour voters are much more likely to read the *Sun* or the *Daily Record* than *The Herald* or *The Daily Telegraph*. In these constituencies at election time Labour will not spend large amounts of resources persuading people to vote Labour. The Labour Party knows most people, if they vote, will vote Labour. The task is more one of motivating core voters to actually vote.

Likewise, the Conservatives know that their core vote lies within the middle classes who are employed in the private sector. Core Conservative voters are more likely to live in suburban areas, especially in the Southern Home Counties, within commuting distance of London. They will read newspapers such as the *Daily Mail* or *The Daily Telegraph*. Like Labour, they cannot take this voter for granted, but they know this voter is an instinctive Conservative and will not need much per-

The Conservatives' core voters are middle class

suading. The task, as for Labour, is to motivate their core voters to actually vote.

The Liberal Democrats know that their core vote lies in the educated, *Guardian*-reading, middle classes who work in the public sector. They care about the environment and international affairs, and want better public services and equal opportunities.

Historically, the Liberal Democrats' problem has been that these voters are not concentrated in any one geographical area. This means that, under the first-past-the-post (FPTP) voting system, it is more difficult for the Liberal Democrats to win seats. For this reason the Liberal Democrats have had to target a certain number of 'winnable seats' where they are placed second and encourage 'tactical voting' to unseat the Labour or Conservative MP.

The SNP's core vote is in the north-east of Scotland and is mostly rural. The SNP has not been able to make any substantial inroads into seats in Scotland's central belt. The SNP has high hopes of making a breakthrough into Labour heartlands at the 2007 Scottish Parliament elections.

Floating Voters

Because the FPTP voting system rewards parties with strong regional bases, there are many 'safe' parliamentary seats. Therefore, it is the 'swing' or 'marginal' seats which will decide the outcome of an election.

These are seats with significant numbers of middle-class or 'new' working-class voters. These voters are not loyal to any single political party. They vote on issues. They weigh up their options. Which party will improve education? Which party will improve the NHS? Which party can lower my mortgage or make my house go up in value? Which party will tax me less or spend my taxes more wisely?

Psephologists (the term used for those who study voting behaviour) regularly come up with new terms to identify such people at each general election.

In 1997, the time of Labour's landslide general election victory, the term was 'Mondeo Man'. Prior to Tony Blair's leadership, Mondeo Man had voted

Mondeo Man was from a working-class background and had voted Labour when he was younger, but he had moved up in the world.

Conservative. He was from a working-class background and had voted Labour when he was younger, but he had moved up in the world. He had bought a house, invested in shares and bought a nice family car, such as the Ford Mondeo.

To Tony Blair, here was living proof that Labour had to change. This was evidence that the public associated Labour only with the poor. These days, the majority of people in the UK are not poor.

Blair concluded that Labour could only form a government if it appealed to the economically successful, as well as to the poor—the 'haves' as well as the 'have nots'. It was simple arithmetic. Labour changed its policies becoming, in the process, 'New Labour'. Mondeo man came back. In 2005 Labour, for the first time in the Party's history, won three general elections in a row.

New Britain New Voting

A good conclusion would be that social class as an influence on voting has not gone away. For example, at the 2005 general election, Labour won 45% of the vote from social classes D and E. This can be compared to the Conservatives' 21% from within these groups.

By contrast, at the top of the social ladder, 37% of classes A and B voted Conservative, while 32% voted Labour.

The influence of social class these days is just more sophisticated and complex than in the past.

Sadly, especially under the FPTP voting system, social classes D and E are the voters to whom no party pays much attention. They mostly vote Labour, if at all. If they are concentrated, as they usually are, in a very safe Labour seat, Labour is more likely to target its resources on more marginal seats where its candidates are under pressure. Perhaps as a result Labour's share of the vote from classes D and E fell from 58% to 45%, with the Liberal Democrats making the most ground within this group of voters.

The battleground in elections today is over the new working and middle classes, codenamed 'hard-working families'. Their vote floats. If these voters also happen to live in a marginal seat, they will be the subject of a great deal of attention by all the major political parties.

This has led to a new criticism of the FPTP voting system, namely that some voters are more influential than others. If you are middle class (more likely to vote and more likely to switch your vote) and live in a marginal seat (have a greater incentive to vote) your views are more likely to be listened to than those of a poor person living in a deprived housing estate, whose Labour vote could be taken (mistakenly perhaps) for granted.

GENDER AND VOTING BEHAVIOUR

In 2005, women became the targets of attention for party strategists. Women used to have a strong attachment to the Conservatives. In fact, if it had not been for the female vote, Labour probably would have won every post-war general election up until 1979.

Since then though, women's votes have been more fluid. However, the influence of gender on voting behaviour should not be seen as distinct from social class. It is middle class women who are sought after. Meet 'School Gate Mum'.

School Gate Mum

School Gate Mum is the British version of the 'Soccer Mums' found in the USA. She is a working woman who has a demanding life, balancing work and family responsibilities. She is the pivotal member of that broad section of the population described as 'hard-working families'. She will be either 'new working class' or a professional, middle- class person.

School Gate Mum will work and pay taxes. She will care about 'quality of life' issues such as smoking bans, child benefits and childcare. She will want flexibility in her working life and will look to enjoy her spare time either at family-friendly outings or to have the money to enjoy the company of her 'girlie' friends—shopping and socialising.

School Gate Mum is not ideological. In fact, she does not see herself as political at all and will rarely read the current affairs sections of newspapers, far less watch 'heavy' news programmes. Nevertheless, she does care about the state of her community and the wider country. She will discuss social issues at the school gate or in the office and she is very likely to vote. For these reasons, every political party is looking for her support.

In 2005, women's votes were critical to Labour's success. According to MORI, 38% of women voted Labour, 32% voted Conservative and 22% voted Liberal Democrat. By comparison, men voted equally for Labour and the Conservatives (34%), with 23% voting Liberal Democrat.

If women only had voted, Labour would have won a Commons majority of 90, rather than the 66 it did manage. If only men had voted, Tony Blair would have a majority of only 24 backbenchers.

AGE AND VOTING BEHAVIOUR

The old cliché says that as you get older you become more conservative. Or, 'if you're not a socialist at twenty you have no heart. If you're still a socialist at forty you have no brain'.

At the 2005 general election, the Liberal Democrats did well among young people. They won the Hansard school mock elections. Labour still did well among younger voters, but not as well as in 1997, when the 'youthful' appeal of Tony Blair and the 'things can only get better' campaign was very influential.

The only social group that has remained solidly Conservative is older voters, with the over-65s (and indeed over-55s) giving the Conservatives a consistent 6% to 10% lead in opinion polls. Maybe the old cliché has some truth in it. At the 2005 general election, elderly celebrity Joan Collins campaigned for the UK Independence Party, which places itself to the Right of the Conservatives on most issues.

RACE AND VOTING BEHAVIOUR

Black voters are significantly more likely to be Labour supporters, as are Asian voters, although not as strongly as black voters.

This could be back to the class relationship again, with black people more likely to have a low income and to live in poorer inner city areas. Labour, in general, has a better image with ethnic minority voters. When many black and Asian people arrived in the UK at the end of the 1960s, the Conservatives were identified as being anti-immigrant by minority groups.

William Hague, Conservative leader at the 2001 general election tried to make immigration an issue. This alienated black and Asian voters. David Cameron has tried to end the Conservatives' image as being anti-immigration and has made serious efforts to portray the Conservative Party as an inclusive party for all sections of the community.

Scotland has a much smaller number of ethnic minority voters than other parts of the UK. This situation may change if the influx of new Europeans, especially Poles, continues. The Polish vote may well become significant in future elections in Scotland.

These days, the influence of race is very closely connected to religion.

RELIGION AND VOTING BEHAVIOUR

Historically, religion was a big factor in Scottish elections. The Conservative Party, the only party ever to win over 50% of the vote in Scotland, made successful appeals to 'Protestant' working-class voters, portraying Labour as the party of poor Catholic Irish immigrants.

The influence of religion has declined in the post-war years. It does, nevertheless, retain an influence in Scotland, as the SNP has found it difficult to break Labour's support among Catholic West of Scotland voters.

The SNP has made a calculated effort to widen its appeal and attract Catholic support, for example by backing denominational schooling. The Party therefore was overjoyed in 2006 when Cardinal Keith O'Brien spoke of the benefits of independence.

This does not mean that Scotland's Roman Catholics will now automatically vote SNP because their leader is supportive of independence. The link between religion and voting has been in decline for some time. However, Scottish Labour is taking the Cardinal's views seriously, with senior Party figures entering 'damage limitation' talks with the Church.

Outside Christianity Muslim voters, who in the past have been relatively faithful Labour supporters, have turned away from the party over Tony Blair's support for the war in Iraq and over other issues related to the war on terror.

In 2005, George Galloway, who had left the Labour Party and created his own party, famously won the seat of Bethnal Green in London, with its high Asian population. The seat had previously been held by leading Labour MP Oona King.

Key Issue:
Does the media influence the way people vote?

THE MEDIA AND VOTING BEHAVIOUR

Like all the other factors, the relationship between the media and voting behaviour is a complex one which should not be simplified.

A common error is accepting that all voters believe everything they read in newspapers and simply vote for the particular party 'their' newspaper supports. For example, at the 1997 general election was it really 'The Sun wot won it' or was it the case that the previously Conservative-supporting *Sun* newspaper like everyone

else simply saw which way the tide was turning and jumped ship to support Labour?

The media must have some influence on voters. The support of newspapers is important to politicians. Tony Blair would not be so keen to have friendly relations with Rupert Murdoch (owner of BskyB and the *Sun*) if the media had no influence. Political parties would not spend so much time and energy on 'spin' if the information people see on television and read in newspapers had no influence on how they vote.

The key issue is what that influence is. Does the media shape people's beliefs? Or does it merely reinforce existing beliefs? Or can it alone change people's ideas?

What is not in doubt is that political parties are proactive in getting their message across in the media, rather than taking the chance of being misrepresented. Professional 'spin doctors', most famously Alastair Campbell, are employed by the political parties to present information in the most favourable light possible.

'Off-message' politicians or maverick candidates are kept well away from the media. Instead, good communicators and politicians seen to be popular with the voters are pushed to the fore by the parties.

Most politicians these days are disciplined and trained media professionals. Pagers and Blackberry mobile phones keep candidates up-to-date with the latest 'line' from party headquarters.

In modern elections, the media rarely catches a politician off guard. The exception to this was John Prescott who punched a protester during the 2001 general election campaign. Did the headline 'Two Jabs' in the following day's *Sun* really do him, or the Labour Party, any damage? Some people may have thought 'I'm not voting for that thug', but others may have thought 'Nice one! I like that guy!' It sums up the nature of this topic. We cannot really be certain what the influence the media has on any individual voter. What repels one voter, may attract another.

Television and the Internet are replacing the tabloid media as a source of news. Television is much more balanced. On the other hand, the vast range of websites, blogs and chat rooms can present whatever version of the truth the voter wants to hear!

The tabloid coverage of politics can still be highly partisan. The *Daily Mirror* front page in 2005 showed Michael Howard, who was Conservative leader at the time, as Dracula, clutching a lump of wood to his bosom.

The *Sun* stopped short of the big Vote Blair campaigns of 1997 and 2001, taking a much more neutral headline of 'Give Blair a Kick in the Ballots'. On the other hand, the *Daily Mail* urged voters to give Tony Blair a 'bloody nose'.

PARTY LEADERS AND VOTING BEHAVIOUR

In these days of obsession with celebrities, the personal image of leaders is becoming more important. Some analysts speak of an 'electoral cycle'. A party leader with the right message can touch the emotions of the voters. It is their time.

Margaret Thatcher did it with 'Labour isn't working' in 1979. The Tories were in power for eighteen years. Tony Blair captured the mood of the people with 'New' Labour and 'things can only get better' in 1997. The SNP had its greatest days in the 1970s with 'Its Scotland's Oil' campaign. The Conservatives' David Cameron has led Tony Blair in the opinion polls yet is searching for that elusive soundbite and key message which can end Labour's dominance.

APATHY

Lastly, let us not forget that not voting is a form of voting behaviour too. UK general elections rarely achieve more than two-thirds of voters turning out to vote. Even the historic 1999 Scottish Parliament elections drew only 62% of voters to the polls.

Why do so many people choose not to vote? Is it laziness? Are the political parties too similar? With all parties chasing the 'big tent', do people now feel that voting will not make any difference?

This theory does not hold much credibility in Scotland where parties as diverse as the Scottish Socialists and the Conservatives stand candidates in every constituency.

Does the FPTP voting system with its safe seats alienate voters? If you know who is going to win, why vote? On the other hand, maybe voters are happy with the current government and not voting is a sign of contentment? Is it the case that with modern life so frantic, people are simply too busy?

In 2007, elections for Scottish local government will be carried out using the Single Transferable Vote (STV). It will be interesting to see if voter turnout increases with this system and which parties win or lose from it.

Would including a 'none of the above' option on the voting papers give voters a positive chance to express their views?

Is ICT the way ahead? Would introducing text or electronic voting, as used in television shows such as the X factor, encourage more people to vote?

Would lowering the voting age to 16 encourage more people to get into the habit of voting?

Study Theme 2:
Wealth and Health Inequalities in the UK

Reference to the Pulse Publications textbook *UK Social Issues* (second edition), Chapters 1, 3, 4, 5, 6, 7, and 8 and www.modernityscotland.co.uk will enhance the use of these revision notes. It is assumed that you have studied the course and have a sound understanding of the key social and economic issues surrounding inequalities in the UK.

EXAM REQUIREMENTS

You are expected to display knowledge and understanding of:

1   Evidence of inequalities in wealth and health; causes of inequalities in wealth and health; consequences of inequalities in wealth and health.

2   With reference to ethnicity and gender: the extent of social and economic inequalities; the nature and effect of government responses to deal with these inequalities.

3   The principles of the Welfare State. The debate over the provision of and funding of health care and welfare; individual and collective responsibility.

Key issue:
To what extent should the welfare state or the individual take responsibility for health and economic quality of life?

INDIVIDUALISTS V COLLECTIVISTS

Individualists are sometimes referred to as being 'right wing'. Individualists believe that people themselves must provide solutions to society's problems. The Conservative Party has, traditionally, been more sympathetic to individualist views.

Take bad health or health inequalities for example. Individualists believe it is a person's choice to smoke, drink or take drugs. It is their fault and no one else's if they fall ill. Individualists believe that health education in schools, and government campaigns and laws to promote healthy living are sufficient to allow individuals to take responsibility for their health. Individualists believe that people should have the right to spend their money the way they want. If someone chooses to spend money on cigarettes, they should pay the consequences themselves and not blame anyone else for their poor health.

By contrast, if an individual chooses to save his/her money, s/he should not have to pay extra taxes for services to treat those who squander their income. Those who choose to look after their health by keeping fit or even by buying private health care, should not have to pay higher taxes for those who make 'bad' lifestyle choices.

Collectivists, on the other hand, look to society as a whole for explanations for bad health or health inequalities. The Labour Party, traditionally, has been more collectivist in its approach.

Collectivists would point to poor parenting or peer group pressure leading individuals to make bad choices. They would explain inequalities by the pressures and stresses of living on a low income which can lead to low self-esteem and poor prospects. This, they claim, causes people to make short-term, 'live for today' decisions, because they do not have hope in the long term.

The collectivists' response is for the state to invest in education, housing and job creation to enable individuals to have a ladder of opportunity and have an incentive to make healthier lifestyle decisions.

Few people today are complete individualists or complete collectivists. The major political parties fall into the centre ground where the debate is over the extent to which it is the state or the individual who takes responsibility.

In the early years of the welfare state, the balance was towards the collectivists. There was a political reaction to this approach and the individualist Conservatives took power for many years.

New Labour has selected ideas from both the collectivist and the individualist approaches to create the so-called 'third way solution'.

THE WELFARE STATE

The welfare state we know today is a product of World War Two. Before the war, there were great class divisions and inequalities. Health care, for example, had to be paid for and many poor people dreaded being ill. The country required great national unity to defeat the Nazis and there was the feeling that a similar collectivist effort was required to rebuild the country.

A Labour government was elected which pledged to nationalise the main industries of the country. The Labour government put into place the ideas of a Liberal, Sir William Beveridge, who envisaged social care from the cradle to the grave. Beveridge identified five giant evils in society:

- bad housing (squalor),
- poor public health (disease),
- unemployment (idleness),
- lack of education (ignorance) and
- poverty (want).

These evils were to be tackled in a collective way, by the whole country together. Individuals would pay a special tax, called national insurance, which would act as a national insurance policy against becoming ill or unemployed, or being old. The state would provide solutions to the social evils of the country.

The National Health Service (NHS) was established to tackle poor health. Council houses were built to improve housing. In the 1970s comprehensive schools were built to improve educational standards. Industries were nationalised to allow the government to keep unemployment low. A wide range of benefits were established as a 'safety net' if people lost their job.

The Individualist Challenge

The Conservative governments of 1979–1997 turned Beveridge's collectivist idea on its head. Instead of the state providing collective solutions, Prime Minister Margaret Thatcher (opposite)

sought individual solutions. Nationalised industries, such as British Steel, were privatised. Individuals were encouraged to buy shares in these companies.

The NHS was not privatised, but its 'hotel' services, such as cleaning and catering, were. Hospitals now had to publish data on the success of their operations, the so-called 'death tables', to allow patient choice. This choice, it was believed, would drive up standards.

Schools were not privatised, but the 'parents charter' allowed parents to shop around for the best school for their children. Children no longer had to go to the local school. Statistics on exam results were published. Parent power, it was believed, would force schools to raise standards – or close.

Perhaps the biggest revolution came in housing under 'Right to Buy' legislation. The state, in the form of local authorities, had to sell council houses to tenants if the tenant wished to buy. Houses in desirable areas were bought, often at discounted prices way below market value. Local authorities were left with little housing stock for local people who could not afford to buy. Those houses that were left tended to be in deprived communities.

A WELFARE STATE FOR THE TWENTY FIRST CENTURY

It is in this context that the New Labour government, which came to power in 1997, sought to 'modernise' the welfare state. Previous Labour governments had tackled the social evils—bad housing, poor education, unemployment, poverty and poor health by collectivism. This time, 'New' Labour would not take the collectivist approach.

Modern political and economic challenges

The 'new middle classes' want to have their cake and eat it. Many people today expect high quality public services, but they do not want to pay more taxes. New Labour had to promise not to raise taxes.

Socially, the country had moved on in other ways. In 1945 Beveridge lived in a society where average life expectancy was around 65. The government did not expect to pay pensions to people for very long. Today, all this has changed. Average life expectancy today is around 77 for men and 81 for women. It is expected to rise as medical science finds new cures, the public become better educated and public health improves. In the past, over 13,000 Scots died every year from tobacco use—the equivalent of 250 a week or 35 a day. Scotland's ban on smoking in public places is expected to save thousands of lives.

Money, therefore, has to be found to pay for pensions and health care for the increasing number of elderly people in our society.

At the same time, the birth rate has dropped. In Beveridge's day people, generally, had two or three children. Now, people are getting married later, or not at all. More people are choosing to live alone, or to have fewer children later in life. Some are choosing to have no children at all.

All this amounts to a 'demographic timebomb'. More people are relying on state care, but there are fewer workers who pay taxes and national insurance to fund it.

Society's values have moved on too. In Beveridge's day, divorce was difficult. There was shame about being a 'lone parent'. Now there are many lone parents and the state has to provide support.

Few women had careers in Beveridge's day. Now women have equal rights with men and many women want a career as well as a family.

People can no longer rely on a 'job for life'. We now live in a global economy. Low skilled jobs can be exported to the Third World, where pay is lower. The jobs which are left in the UK increasingly require skills and enterprising attitudes which were not required in 1945.

Division and Inequality

Under the individualist approach the giant evils remained. Many people became proud homeowners for the first time, but there were now 'ghetto estates', the areas no one wanted to buy housing in, where there were high crime rates and drug abuse.

Some schools became 'magnet schools' with well-behaved and motivated pupils, and the good exam results which followed. Waiting lists were created, fraudulent addresses even made up, to get into these sought after schools. At the other extreme, there were 'failing schools', which the new middle class had deserted, and which often had to close completely.

There were divisions and inequalities in health care too. The difference in life expectancy between the rich and the poor grew. The well-off educated classes, who acted on government advice, lived longer. The new 'socially excluded', with low self-esteem and poor prospects, opted for unhealthy lifestyle choices.

The gap between rich and poor grew. Those in well-paid work did well. Low taxes and the property boom allowed many people, some for the first time, to afford houses, cars, shares, regular holidays abroad and all the benefits success under capitalism can bring.

Those left behind, the 'have nots', became more left behind. Industries which Scotland, especially, depended upon, such as mining and manufacturing, lost thousands of jobs. Entire towns and villages changed from being bustling, thriving communities to being ghost towns where only the elderly and the poor remained.

Unemployment remained high in the Conservative years and the options for the unskilled and demotivated were low paid work or years of dependency on benefits.

A Sharper Focus to the Welfare State

New Labour's overall approach is often referred to as the 'third way'. New Labour felt it had to tackle the divisions in society, but 'tough' choices would have to be made. There would be rights for the unemployed, but responsibilities too.

The state would continue to support those in need, but they had to be in genuine need. Those who could work would be expected to. The state would help them to find work, rather than relying on benefits.

Some of the old collectivist approach remained within Tony Blair's governments, in that the government has taken the lead in tackling the social evils. Nevertheless, there is also some of the individualist ways of Margaret Thatcher. The individual is expected to take responsibility for seizing opportunities to become more independent of the government.

As former Minister for Work and Pensions, David Blunkett, said:

> "The welfare state of the twenty first century will not simply be a safety net, but an enabler—a ladder out of poverty".

This 'third way' approach represents the state helping, but the individual contributing, with the ultimate aim of making the new generation more financially independent.

New Labour hopes it can save money by 'targeting benefits' at those most in need. Instead of increasing certain benefits for all, the government has introduced 'tax credits' which are means-tested benefits, available only to those below a certain income level.

Pension Credits mean that the most needy pensioners receive higher pensions than those with savings and assets.

Child benefit remains, but is one of the few 'universal' (everyone gets it) benefits left.

The Child Trust Fund is a classic New Labour approach. All new parents are given money (low income groups receive more) to open bank accounts for their children. The money can grow in a bank account until the child is eighteen. During this time, parents or grandparents can add extra money.

To some extent therefore, New Labour has retained the 'old values' of the welfare state. The most vulnerable in society will be looked after, but the government provides a 'hand up', not a 'hand out'.

Welfare to Work

New Labour believes that the best way out of poverty is work. Welfare to work is an umbrella term, which covers a wide variety of policies designed to have people working, rather than living on benefits.

The New Deals are one way. Those out of work now need to register with Jobcentre Plus. A Gateway adviser will help an unemployed person find a New Deal which is appropriate. There is a New Deal for Lone Parents, a New Deal for Young People (18–24-year-olds), a New Deal for people aged 25+, a New Deal for those aged 50+, a New Deal for the Disabled, and so on.

The New Deal can be a college course. It can be a temporary job with a company. It can be voluntary work with a charity or a non-governmental organisation. All New Deals come with training, so if the person does not find work right away, the training and qualifications will mean the experience has not been a waste of time and job prospects will be enhanced.

New Labour introduced the National Minimum Wage (NMW). In the past many people would be worse off working because they would lose benefits such as housing or council tax benefits. New Labour wanted to give people an incentive to work, so the NMW was brought in and has been increased several times since 1998.

CRITICISMS OF NEW LABOUR

Not everyone believes that the New Labour approach has been a success. The government has been attacked by the political Left and the political Right.

The Left (collectivists) believe that the government has given with one hand and taken away with the other. For example, a person who gets a job paying the National Minimum Wage may lose out on free school meals or have their Council Tax rebate taken away.

Others believe that more benefits, such as free school meals or free prescriptions should be available to all, regardless of income. They would argue that if the government can afford a war in Iraq, it can afford free school meals or prescriptions.

Those on the Right (individualists) believe that the government has not done enough to tackle 'dependency'. They claim that there are still many people, for example on Incapacity Benefit, who could be working but are not. They would like the government to get tougher with 'scroungers'. They claim that 'hard-working families' pay too much tax which goes to fund health care for people who choose to make 'bad' lifestyle choices such as alcohol and drug abuse.

Those on the Right criticise the 'nanny state', claiming that the government still interferes too much in people's lives. They criticise 'nagging' campaigns on healthy living. The ban on smoking in enclosed public places is, they claim, an attack on individual rights.

They would also claim that New Labour has broken its promise not to raise taxes. While the 22% rate has not been increased, many more people, not necessarily so-called 'fat cats', now earn enough to pay 40% on some of their earnings. Indirect taxes have also gone up. Taxes on fuel, alcohol and tobacco have all increased.

INEQUALITIES IN SOCIETY: HEALTH

The National Health Service (NHS) aims to treat all patients equally on the basis of need. However, despite almost sixty years of NHS care, widespread health inequalities remain.

Geography

Scotland lies at the bottom of the life expectancy league. An Office of National Statistics report in 2004 showed that eight out of the ten local authorities with the lowest life expectancy in the UK were in Scotland. Glasgow is the only city in the UK where male life expectancy is below 70 (69.1 years in Glasgow). Within Glasgow, the Shettleston constituency in the city's east end has the worst figure for men at 63 years—lower than in war-torn Bosnia, Lebanon and the Gaza Strip. The health gap is, in fact, growing. Figures published by the Office for National Statistics in 2006 showed that women living in Chelsea could expect to live 12.3 years longer than women in Glasgow. Eight Scottish local authorities were among the lowest ten UK local authorities for male life expectancy. For women, the worst five areas for female life expectancy were in Scotland.

To some extent geography on its own can affect your health. Where you live can affect the treatment you receive from the NHS. The 'postcode lottery' is a much used phrase. Different health boards have different rules regarding access to treatment. Expensive treatments, such as fertility treatment, may be free in one part of the country, but not in another.

A shortage of NHS dentists has been a particular problem in rural areas of Scotland. An investigation by *The Sunday Times* in January 2004 found that there was not one dentist in the whole of Dumfries and Galloway who could take on a new NHS patient. The Scottish Executive has introduced cash incentives for dentists to set up practices in more remote areas of the country.

A study published in July 2006 by the National Dental Inspection programme found that:
- children living in deprived communities are twice as likely to suffer from tooth decay as those in wealthier areas.
- 64% of children from deprived areas had decay in their permanent teeth by Primary 7 age compared with only 30% of children in the wealthiest parts of Scotland.

A 2006 NHS survey revealed that North Lanarkshire, one of Scotland's poorest areas with the third lowest female life expectancy and the seventh lowest male life expectancy, has the fewest doctors.

It can therefore be seen that poverty, rather than geography, is the main cause of health inequalities. Poor people live in poor places.

New Labour has made ending health inequalities a major policy goal.

Still Dead Poor

There is a vast body of evidence to show the links between poverty and ill health. A survey of health inequalities, *People and Places*, was carried out in 2001. It revealed a widening gap between rich and poor. The percentage of the country's wealth held by the top 10% increased from 47% to 54% between 1997 and 2004 according to the Institute for Public Policy Research.

The UK's great Northern cities, Glasgow, Liverpool and Manchester, which thrived during the days of the Empire, are in decline. They are poorer and their populations are declining. 41% of Glasgow's households live in poverty.

Glasgow is not alone. West Dunbartonshire, Dundee, North Lanarkshire and Inverclyde are all to be found in the top twenty of the UK's poorest areas.

Another UK survey, the National Shoppers survey, found that the five poorest places to live in the UK are all in Scotland. Cumnock, Bellshill, Kirkcaldy, Clydebank and Irvine all had the highest numbers of socially excluded households.

Kirkcaldy, in Fife, had 15% of its residents living on a monthly household income of less than £400.

Within Scotland, the health figures are equally stark. People in Glasgow's Maryhill are more than twice as likely to die of heart disease as those living in Edinburgh West.

In Anniesland in Glasgow, nearly 40% of pregnant women smoked, compared to 10% in affluent Eastwood in East Renfrewshire.

The highest life expectancy in Scotland is to be found in North East Fife (77.6 years on average). Men in East Dorset can expect to live until they are 80. Women in Kensington and Chelsea can normally expect to live until they are 84.8.

Health Inequalities in Edinburgh

Glasgow is often used to show that health inequalities exist within a city. However, the problem is not simply an east/west one of geography. There are also widespread inequalities within Edinburgh.

An *Edinburgh Evening News* investigation in 2005 revealed that a girl growing up in the affluent Fairmilehead district can expect to live until she is 89. By contrast, a girl growing up on the city's Craigmillar es-

tate has, on average, a life expectancy of just 70. A person living in Muirhouse or West Pilton is nearly four times as likely to die of cancer as someone living in Comiston or the Braid Hills.

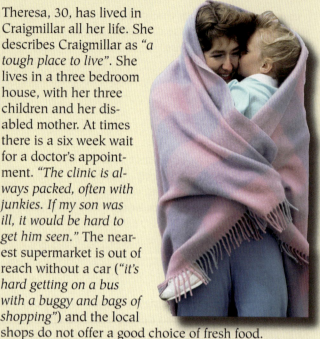

Theresa, 30, has lived in Craigmillar all her life. She describes Craigmillar as *"a tough place to live"*. She lives in a three bedroom house, with her three children and her disabled mother. At times there is a six week wait for a doctor's appointment. *"The clinic is always packed, often with junkies. If my son was ill, it would be hard to get him seen."* The nearest supermarket is out of reach without a car (*"it's hard getting on a bus with a buggy and bags of shopping"*) and the local shops do not offer a good choice of fresh food.

Alison, 46, who lives in Fairmilehead, has a different story to tell. She has access to a wide variety of supermarkets. Alison is well informed about health issues. *"I've been making a conscious decision to buy a lot more organic. Although it's a bit more expensive, I think it's worth it."* Her family house is a detached bungalow, with a large garden, at the bottom of the Pentland hills. She says, *"I'm not surprised this area has a high life expectancy. I walk most places and my kids do too. We've got excellent access to health care. It's such a nice place to live."*

62% of men and 54% of women in Scotland are overweight or obese.

Problem drinking is increasingly taking its toll too. It affects all of us in Scotland, but the class inequalities are stark. Glasgow Govan had 1,664 alcohol-related admissions to hospital per 100,000 people. By contrast, Dunfermline West had 'just' 868 alcohol-related admissions.

HOW DO WE ADDRESS HEALTH INEQUALITIES?

This depends on your analysis of the problem. A balanced conclusion would be that to some extent, poverty is to blame, but perhaps individuals need to take responsibility too.

From an individualist perspective, health inequalities can be explained by people's own behaviour. Yes, there are links with poverty, but not all poor people smoke, take drugs or abuse alcohol. No one forces people to lead unhealthy lives. From the Left, collectivists blame the stress of living on low incomes leading people into destructive behaviour. There are also issues of lack of access to health care, sporting opportunities and healthy foods. Damp and cold housing are contributory factors too.

The Scottish Executive is taking a 'holistic approach' to solving health inequalities. It does not believe that financial initiatives like giving poorer people money to buy fresh food will solve the problem.

Work

Both the Scottish Executive and the UK government believe that the root cause of poverty is a lack of work.

This is why initiatives such as the UK government's National Minimum Wage and the New Deals are important. Although having a regular wage is an important factor, the psychological 'feel good' effect of doing an enjoyable job can help people to live healthier lives too.

Housing

The Scottish Executive is trying to improve housing and the environment in which people live. New housing associations, such as the Glasgow Housing Association, are being formed to modernise the city's housing stock.

School intervention

The Executive is also encouraging healthier foods and drinks in schools. It is funding breakfast clubs and 'early intervention' initiatives such as facilities for brushing young children's teeth in primary schools.

Smoking

Scotland's flagship health initiative is the ban on smoking in enclosed public places. The intention is not just to cut back on 'passive smoking' which used to occur in pubs and clubs, but to encourage smokers to give up altogether.

The stark facts are that smokers are now concentrated in the poorest parts of our society. Those who can least afford to smoke are smoking the most and it is killing them. Death rates are highest in areas of poverty. In 2005, people living in Easterhouse, Glasgow, spent an average of £584 per year on cigarettes out of an average household income of £16,813. By contrast, those living in Bromley in Kent had an average income of almost £50,000 and the average amount spent on smoking was just £67.

Only 15% of professional males in the UK smoke, compared to 42% of male unskilled workers. 90% of all lung cancer deaths are caused by smoking. Glasgow has the highest rates of smoking in Scotland and the highest rates of lung cancer. 145 out of every 100,000 men in Glasgow are diagnosed with lung cancer every year.

Key issue:
To what extent are there race and gender inequalities in the UK?

INEQUALITIES IN SOCIETY: RACE

The Glass Door

Many of Scotland's ethnic minority workers are employed in low level, poorly paid jobs. Retail and catering are two of the main sectors, often through self-employment, (newsagent or grocery store) or being employed by other ethnic minority employers, e.g. working in restaurants.

A Commission for Racial Equality (CRE) study, carried out between 1980 and 1994 found that white applicants for jobs were twice as likely to be accepted for an interview as either black Caribbean or Asian applicants.

According to the CRE, Scotland's ethnic minority workers are two or three times more likely to be unemployed than white workers.

Ethnic minority workers are not employed in sufficient numbers compared to their number in society in most private sector organisations and in key professions such as teaching, law and social work.

Some people speak, not of the glass ceiling most commonly referred to in relation to gender discrimination, but a 'glass door' for ethnic minority men and women.

Not only are ethnic minority Britons not making it to the top, they are not getting the jobs in the first place. There is also a lack of role models for young people from ethnic minority backgrounds. If they do not see people like themselves in top level jobs they may feel that there is no point in applying for a job in that area, even one lower down the scale. Consequently, no one from an ethnic minority background will work for that company in a job which could lead to promotion to the top.

Racial Harassment

No one was convicted of the murder of waiter Surjit Chhokar (opposite) in Overtown, Lanarkshire in November 1998, after the three men charged blamed each other for the killing during two separate trials. The case has been described as 'Scotland's Stephen Lawrence'. Scotland's top law officer, the Lord Advocate (who was Colin Boyd at the time), admitted that his office had "failed" the family of Surjit Chhokar, when prosecuting the men accused of his murder.

In 2000, Glasgow City Council began taking asylum seekers as part of the UK government's dispersal programme. Over 6,000 were accommodated in some of

Glasgow's poorest communities, such as Castlemilk and Sighthill. According to Strathclyde police, there has been a 60% increase in the number of racist incidents since asylum seekers began to arrive. In August 2001, the murder of Firsat Dag, a Kurdish man, led to violent demonstrations, which the British National Party (BNP) attempted to capitalise on.

There is no doubt that racial tensions have increased further since the 9/11 attacks on America. The 7/7 bombings in London and the plane bombings scare in the summer of 2006 have heightened tensions, usually referred to as 'Islamophobia,' between Muslims and white Britons. There were demands for 'passenger profiling' of air passengers, with some people expressing the extreme view that Asians should not be allowed to fly.

However, there are more positive stories. Islamophobia is clearly not an issue for the Glasgow teenagers known as the 'Glasgow Girls'. The group won the Scottish Campaign of the Year award at the 2005 Scottish Politician of the Year Awards.

The Vucaj family from Albania were asylum seekers who lived in Drumchapel. Nimet and Saida Vucaj attended secondary school, where they made many friends, among them Amal Azzudin. When the Vucaj family's application for asylum was finally rejected by the Home Office, they were forcibly removed from their home in the early hours of the morning. Amal and her friends formed a pressure group to raise awareness of the plight of children of asylum seekers.

The Glasgow Girls met First Minister Jack McConnell to put pressure on the Scottish Executive to reach an agreement with the UK Home Office on humane treatment for failed asylum seekers. An agreement has now been reached. Families of failed asylum seekers have now been given assurances by the Home Office that they will not be deported while their children are sitting exams. While force may still have to be used at times, the so-called 'dawn raids' are to stop. The multiethnic Glasgow girls are a social and political success story.

To some extent, overt racism is easier to deal with. It can be spotted, the perpetrators identified and action taken. Institutionalised racism is more complex.

Institutionalised racism

This phrase came to the public's attention with the murder of Stephen Lawrence (opposite) in London in 1993, the botched police investigation and the subsequent MacPherson Report. MacPherson concluded that there was 'unwitting institutionalised racism' within the Metropolitan Police (usually referred to as 'the

Met'). What does 'unwitting institutionalised racism' mean?

Institutionalised racism occurs when the policies and culture of an organisation disadvantage people from ethnic minority backgrounds. The MacPherson Report defined it as:

> "the collective failure of an organisation to provide an appropriate and professional service to people because of their colour, culture or ethnic origin. It can be seen or detected in processes, attitudes and behaviour which amount to discrimination through unwitting prejudice, ignorance, thoughtlessness and racial stereotyping which disadvantages minority ethnic people."

For example, individual teachers in a school are very unlikely to be overt racists. However, if the school has a number of Muslim children and if it is completely ignorant of Muslim traditions and celebrations such as Ramadan, it may be institutionally racist. An institution can be racist by the things it does not do, as well as the things it does.

In the case of the Metropolitan Police in 1993, the charge was that officers would routinely believe that crime was more of a black issue than a white one. Statistically, a young black male is more likely to be involved in crime.

There are, however, 'lies, damned lies and statistics'. Not all young black males are criminals. It is not the police's job to decide who is a criminal and who is not—that is up to the courts.

As it happened, Stephen Lawrence, a 17-year-old black male, was a normal, well-behaved and law-abiding young man. He was stabbed to death while on his way home from visiting a friend. There was considerable evidence against the four men charged with his murder but the weak Metropolitan Police investigation let crucial evidence slip away. The charge against the Metropolitan Police was that if this had happened to a white man, the investigation would have been more thorough and professional.

The Met accepted MacPherson's findings and acted to root out institutionalised racism. It disciplined officers who were racist in their actions. Education courses were organised for officers and also training in dealing sensitively with potentially racially charged situations. It tried to change the 'canteen culture' of the force by making racist joke telling and stereotyping unacceptable.

MacPherson recommended that the Met should aim to recruit around 8% of its police officers from ethnic minority backgrounds in order to match London's demographic mix. The Met has now made serious efforts to recruit more widely from London's various racial groups.

The National Black Police Association (NBPA), however, feels that the Met is still too quick to discipline officers from ethnic minority backgrounds. PC Gurpal Virdi, a West London PC, was fired by the Met after being falsely accused of sending hate mail to his colleagues. He won his job back at an industrial tribunal. The NBPA feels that the Met has still to win credibility with ethnic minority communities and, as a result, recruiting ethnic minority officers will remain difficult. Amid growing public fears over gun crime, street violence and drugs, not to mention terrorism, it is vital that the Met recruits a racially diverse police force to combat crime effectively.

The CRE feel that the police have, on the whole, acted decisively to tackle institutionalised racism. A survey by the CRE in Scotland in 2003 found that the police, perhaps because of the public attention in London, were making real efforts, but other public bodies, in particular schools and health authorities, had been slow to improve their procedures and take racial equality seriously.

Government Anti-Racism Initiatives

Overt racial discrimination (i.e. name calling, bullying, refusal of jobs) has been illegal since the *Race Relations Act* of 1976. This law makes it illegal to discriminate in jobs, housing, and public services on the basis of a person's ethnic background, although amazingly the police service was, at the time, omitted from this Act. It also makes it illegal for a person or a group of people to 'promote' racial hatred.

The updated *Race Relations Act* of 2000 now includes the police as well as having certain other new features. The onus is now on both the public and private sectors to show they are proactive in promoting good race relations, rather than waiting for racial equality controversies to appear suddenly.

Large companies now set targets for increasing the number of people from ethnic minority backgrounds whom they employ. Care is also taken over the way the company goes about its business, from its advertising and public image, to recruitment and promotion procedures. This will include even looking at the social

events a company may hold in case some groups are unconsciously excluded. Muslims do not drink alcohol, so if the only social event a company holds has a strong alcohol focus, this could exclude people within the organisation from networking opportunities.

Success of government action

To some extent, legislation against racism has made a difference. The *Race Relations Act* makes potentially racist employers think twice before acting in a racist manner. It also creates a legal framework which provides an opportunity for victims to seek justice through, for example, industrial tribunals.

The 1976 Act created the Commission for Racial Equality (CRE). The CRE is available to help businesses and organisations have fairer employment practices. It will provide victims of racism with legal help. It also plays a wider educational role,  especially among young people. The 'Show Racism the Red Card' football initiative is a good example of the CRE's work.

Overt discrimination is, of course, very damaging to those who receive it. Racial harassment, even if it is 'low level' in the form of so-called jokes or name calling, can be very hurtful, especially to children.

The *Crime and Disorder Act* 1998 has a section for 'racially aggravated' offences or so-called 'hate crimes'. Physical harassment is a serious crime and a genuine problem in certain parts of the country. In the summer of 2001, fuelled by tensions relating to unemployment and poverty, there were race riots in four English cities.

The Scottish Executive's One Scotland campaign tries to tackle racism in Scotland. This is being done mostly by education but also through public information, which enables minority groups to become aware of their rights under the law.

INEQUALITIES IN SOCIETY: GENDER

"Almost thirty years since the Sex Discrimination Act was passed, women are still under-represented in positions of influence in Britain."
(Julie Mellor, Chair of the Equal Opportunities Commission, 2004)

Girls perform much better than boys in secondary education. In general, they behave better and are more interested in learning, so as a result they do much better in exams. If this is the case, why are men still in the top jobs and why are men still earning more than women?

Evidence released by the Equal Opportunities Commission (EOC) in 2005 showed that women in full-time employment earned 19.5% less than men, not 18% as previously thought. In the previous six years, this pay gap had only closed by 1.7%.

The figures also show that the pay gap between males and females starts as early as the teenage years and goes all the way into old age. 14% of 16–17-year-old males worked in better paid manufacturing jobs, while their female counterparts worked in lower paid public service jobs.

At work, women hold less than 10% of the top jobs in education, the police, law and trade unions. The situation in the private sector among the top FTSE 100 companies was no different.

This pay gap means that women retire with less savings and poorer pension plans than men.

Why are there Gender Inequalities?

Girls are out-performing boys at school for a number of reasons. Girls' earlier emotional maturity is the reason most commonly given. Girls, on the whole, tend to realise much earlier than boys that education is vital for any kind of career advancement.

Peer pressure is another reason. The things most teenage boys value in one another—being good at football, being 'a laugh', or fooling around are activities which are at odds with the formal education system. Girls meanwhile, who tend to value academic success and achievement, can meet the challenges of education more easily. Poorer school grades among boys is a global problem and not one which just affects boys in Scotland or the UK.

When boys are taken away from the comfort zone of school, and the reality of working for a living kicks in, they are more likely to achieve their potential. Therefore, a process of catching up is perhaps inevitable.

The glass ceiling

Sex discrimination in employment is illegal. There are powerful laws to make sure employers offer equal opportunities in the hiring and promotion of staff. How-

ever, it is still the woman, rather than the man in a relationship, who is more likely to take time out from work to bring up a baby or look after elderly relatives. That is not because the man is necessarily a sexist. On the contrary, modern man appears to be keener than ever to do his fatherly duties. The answer lies in economics. Because the man in a relationship is more likely to be in the better paid job, it makes financial sense for the woman, rather than the man to give up work. This then creates a vicious circle.

When women give up their jobs, they miss out on the training courses, the networking, the 'away day' bonding with employers, the work experience—all the things that lead to promotion and higher pay. Therefore men are more likely to get the top jobs, therefore women take time off to bring up babies, and the cycle goes on. Until women reach financial equality with men, the glass ceiling is likely to continue.

Gender stereotyping

High earning jobs exist in industries such as IT, science, engineering and construction. These industries have an enduring 'macho' image and attract a much lower number of women. Proving sex discrimination is, however, often difficult. Trades Union Congress (TUC) General Secretary, Brendan Barber claims that
"until more is done to address the images of jobs for the boys and jobs for the girls, the equal pay gap will not go away".

Harassment at work

Domestic violence happens to men too, but it is mostly carried out by men on women. Harassment at work is mostly carried out by men on women. There were 40,000 cases of sex discrimination reported to the EOC in 2001.

Deutsche Bank paid £1,000,000 in damages to investment banker Kay

Swinbourne. A senior manager accused her of sleeping with a male colleague and referred to women as 'hot totty'.

Britain's long hours working culture

British employers have the right to ask their employees to sign a clause opting out of the European Working Time Directive. This sets a limit of forty eight hours a week that staff can work. However, if workers have signed the opt-out clause there is no limit on the number of hours they can work.

Britain's culture of 'presenteeism' (people frightened to go home when their working day is officially over in case they are accused of neglecting their responsibilities) suits men better than women because men are less likely to have family commitments. Men therefore work longer hours and get more pay. Men become more likely to get promotion because they can go 'beyond the call of duty'.

- 39.5% of MSPs are women
- 15% of MPs are women
- 18% of head teachers in Scotland are women
- 10.3% of senior police officers are women

Until more employers introduce flexible working, women in general, though not always, will find it more difficult to attend training courses, network after hours and climb the career ladder.

Government Initiatives to counter Gender Inequalities

It is against the law to discriminate against a person, consciously or unconsciously, on the basis of their gender.

The *Equal Pay Act* means that men and women doing the same or a similar job must be paid the same. Furthermore, men and women must be paid the same if their job is 'of the same value' and where jobs are rated as equivalent. This has been a recent source of conflict between unions representing nursery nurses (overwhelmingly female) and Scotland's local authorities. The trade union UNISON claims that nursery nurses are underpaid compared with other council employees who are doing a job of similar worth.

The *Sex Discrimination Act* and European Human Rights legislation mean not only that employers cannot discriminate against people on account of their gender, but that they must be transparent in showing that they are proactively non-sexist, rather than merely 'treating everyone the same'. For example, application forms and interview procedures must show no gender discrimination whatsoever.

The National Minimum Wage, while not aimed directly at women, has indirectly benefited them more than men as it is women who are more likely to work in low paid jobs.

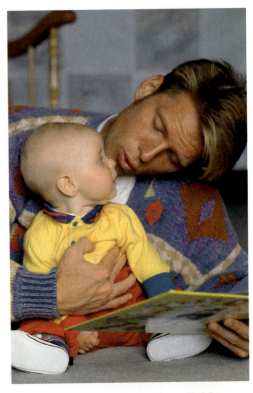

The UK government passed legislation to increase paternity leave to allow men more opportunities to look after their children. The Conservatives in fact are arguing that men should be entitled to a year out of work on full pay in order to care for their children. This is a further attempt to break the glass ceiling.

The government has also adopted a National Childcare Strategy to improve women's access to well-paid work and to try to break the glass ceiling.

Female Success Stories

However, it is not all bad news for women. In certain professions, for example law and medicine, women are beginning to outperform men. In 2006, 65% of entrants to Scottish law courses were women, the highest figure ever.

British Medical Association figures show that 60% of medical students are now female and, for the first time, the number of women registered with the General Medical Council is greater than the number of men. Boys now appear to be more interested in courses such as computing.

In 2006, Elish Angiolini (below) became the first woman to achieve the position of Lord Advocate, Scotland's top legal post. The head of education for the Law Society of Scotland asserted that "by 2010, the typical Scottish lawyer will be under 30, female and from a state school."

Study Theme 3A:
The Republic of South Africa

Reference to the Pulse Publications textbook *Studies in International Relations* (Second edition), South Africa Chapters 9–13 and www.modernityscotland.com will enhance the use of these revision notes. It is assumed that you have studied the course and have a sound understanding of the key political, social and economic issues facing South Africa.

EXAM REQUIREMENTS

You are expected to display knowledge and understanding of:

1   The South African political system: The relationship between the President, National and Provincial Assemblies, and the Constitutional Court.

2   Political Issues: Participation and representation, the role of political parties, media and pressure groups and political trends.

3   Social and Economic Issues: The nature and extent of social and economic inequalities, the effectiveness of government responses and the consequences for different groups.

Key issue:
To what extent is South Africa a successful and stable democracy rather than a country moving towards being a one-party state?

BACKGROUND

South Africa is a multiracial democracy based on a written Constitution which includes a Bill of Rights. The country is a new democracy as it was only in 1994 that the domination of the white minority (the apartheid system ended). In the first free, multiracial elections, Nelson Mandela, leader of the African National Congress (ANC) became the first President of the new 'Rainbow Nation'.

South Africa is the richest country in southern Africa and is the region's 'superpower'. It is rich in natural resources and has a modern manufacturing industry.

Population

South Africa has a population of more than 45 million people made up of the following racial groups:

Black Africans make up 80% of the population with the main tribal groups being Xhosa and Zulu. The black African population is increasing.

The White population is declining and is now less than 10% of the total population. Whites can be divided into two groups—English-speaking and Afrikaners. The Afrikaners ruled the country from 1948–1994 under the policy of apartheid. Many of the Afrikaners are farmers and regard themselves as being the 'white tribe' of South Africa.

Coloureds are of mixed race and, for the first time, the combined coloured and Indian population outnumbers Whites.

South Africa—a political success story?

The 1994 election was a triumph for democracy. The feared inter-tribal war between Inkatha (a Zulu organisation) and the ANC, led by Nelson Mandela, and violence from the extreme White groups did not happen. The country did not descend into anarchy and bloodshed. It was also a triumph for the ANC which won over 60% of the votes in the election. The black majority had finally gained political power.

THE NEW CONSTITUTION

South Africa has a written Constitution which guarantees its people an extensive range of human rights. The Constitution makes clear reference to the need to address the inequalities created by apartheid. Article 9.2 states: "To promote achievement of equality, legislative and other measures designed to protect or advance categories of persons disadvantaged by unfair discrimination may be taken." This has enabled the government to pass legislation which discriminates against Whites.

The Constitution provides for an independent judiciary. The Constitutional Court is the highest court in the land, and deals with the interpretation, protection and enforcement of the Constitution.

> **Important Decisions made by the Constitutional Court**
> - In 2002 the Court ruled in favour of the AIDS Action pressure group Treatment Action Campaign (TAC) and ordered the government to provide an anti-AIDS drug free to HIV/AIDS mothers and children at birth.
> - In 2005 the Court upheld the property rights of white farmers to receive protection from the State if their land was occupied by landless farm labourers.

Government Structure

South Africa has a bicameral parliament consisting of a National Assembly (400 members) and the National Council of Provinces (NCOP), both elected by proportional representation. The President is elected by the National Assembly from among its members and he or she is the executive Head of State and also leads the Cabinet. The President may not serve more than two five-year terms. The dominance of the ANC ensures that the leader of the ANC becomes the President. Thabo Mbeki replaced Nelson Mandela in 1999 and, having won the 2004 election, must stand down in 2009 unless the Constitution is changed.

South Africa is divided into nine provinces, each with its own provincial government. The Constitution offers limited powers to the provinces and their function is to implement the policies of the national government. Local government is finding it difficult to deliver local services such as education and housing.

Political parties

The fact that South Africa has proportional representation (a list system) encourages the participation of a larger number of political parties in the electoral system. Thirty five political parties participated in the 2004 elections and twelve have representatives in the National Assembly.

This electoral system encourages the creation of new parties such as the Independent Democrats, set up in 2003 by Patricia De Lille, a National Assembly Member. The paradox of the electoral system is that it weakens the influence of the main opposition parties as it encourages new parties to be formed. Tony Leon, leader of the Democratic Alliance, called it the "cannibalisation of the opposition".

Below is a brief overview of the main political parties which participated in the 2004 election.

Summary of Political Parties' Manifestos: 2004 Elections

African National Congress (ANC)

Leader: Thabo Mbeki
This party has the overwhelming support of the black African population.

- will create one million jobs through an expanded public works programme;
- through the 2014 plan, reduce unemployment by half;
- will deploy more than 150,000 police on active service;
- will invest more than R15 billion in improving roads and rail transport;
- will speed up Black Economic Empowerment (BEE).

Democratic Alliance (DA)

Leader: Tony Leon
(Sees its role as being an effective and critical opposition.)

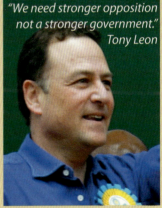

"We need stronger opposition not a stronger government."
Tony Leon

- will provide one million jobs over the next five years by tripling growth rates;
- will speed up privatisation;
- will scrap protective Labour Laws;
- 150,000 police officers on the streets by 2007;
- free anti-AIDS drugs for those living with HIV/AIDS.

Inkatha Freedom Party (IFP)

Leader Chief Buthelezi
Sees its role as defending the traditions of the Zulu nation.

- better trained and resourced police force;
- job creation through government and private investment;
- will promote Black empowerment through agricultural transformation;
- IFP was a member of the Government of National Unity from 1994–2004.

"I am very worried … if we are not careful we are going to have a one-party state."
Chief Buthelezi

The Party has twenty eight seats in the National Assembly. It has thirty two provincial seats with thirty being in KwaZulu-Natal where it shares power with the ANC.

New National Party (NNP)

Leader Marthinus van Schalwyk
The Party disbanded in 2004 and merged with the ANC. Van Schalkwyk became Minister for Tourism.

United Democratic Movement (UDM)

Leader Bantu Holomisa

- The UDM was formed in 1997 by Bantu Holomisa and Roelf Meyer;
- Bantu Holomisa had been expelled from the ANC after accusing a leading party official of corruption;
- Roelf Meyer had been a former white Nationalist Party Cabinet Minister. The new party fought the 1999 election but only won fourteen seats.
- Roelf Meyer retired from politics in 2000. The party draws most of its support from the Eastern Cape (it won six of its nine seats in this province).

Independent Democrats (ID)

Leader Patricia De Lille

- This new party was formed in 2003 under the leadership of Patricia De Lille.
- De Lille was a National Assembly Member for the Pan Africanist Congress (PAC). As an active trade unionist, she has a strong personal following and in a 2004 survey she was found to be the most trusted politician among coloured voters because of her fight against corruption. The ID's policies are similar to the ANC's except on HIV/AIDS where it demands more action.

The party did well in the 2004 election, attracting former NNP supporters. It has seven seats in the National Assembly.

African Christian Democratic Party (ACDP)

Leader Kenneth Meshoe

- The ACDP was formed in 1993 and has participated in all three elections.
- Its aim is to represent South African Christians in Parliament and it has six seats in the National Assembly.

Freedom Front Plus (FFP)

Leader Pieter Mulder

- It sees its role as defending the cultural rights of the Afrikaner people. It has attacked affirmative action as being racist legislation. The party has only four seats in the National Assembly.

Pan Africanist Congress (PAC)

- The PAC was formed in 1959 and offers a radical alternative to the ANC, for example expropriation of land from white farmers. It suffered a major blow when Patricia De Lille left and it has only three seats in the National Assembly.

United Christian Democratic Party (UCDP)

- The UCDP was formed by Lucas Mangope, who during the apartheid era was the head of the 'Homeland of Bophuthatswana'. The party has three national seats and three seats in the North West provincial legislature.

Minority Front (MF)

- The party is led by Amichard Rajbansi and claims to represent the interests of the Indian Community. The MF has two seats in the National Assembly, none in any of the provinces, but has representatives at the local government level in Durban.

Azanian Peoples Organisation (AZAPO)

- AZAPO preaches the philosophy of black consciousness which was associated with Steve Biko, who was killed in police custody in 1977. It has one seat in the National Assembly.

ELECTION RESULTS 1994–2004

A key feature of the election results has been the increase in the ANC's support which rose from 63.1% in 1994 to 69.7% in 2004. The merger of the New National Party (NNP) with the ANC means the ANC now has over 70% of the membership of the National Assembly. In the 2004 election the ANC gained full control of the Western Cape and ended Chief Buthelezi's dominance of KwaZulu-Natal. The Inkatha Freedom Party (IFP) now shares power in the Province with the ANC. For the first time, all seven Provincial Premiers belong to the ANC.

To what extent is South Africa a successful democracy?

Arguments for

1   South Africa is a stable model of democracy for Africa. There have been three peaceful elections based on PR. Thirty five political parties participated in the 2004 elections with twelve parties sitting in the National Assembly. The IFP was in the GNU from 1994–2004.

2   A peaceful transition from Mandela to Mbeki occurred.

3   South Africa has a liberal Constitution guaranteeing freedom to its citizens. It provides for an independent Judiciary. The Constitutional Court ordered Mbeki to provide drugs to combat AIDS.

4   South Africa has a Federal system of government with powers divided between central and provincial governments.

5   There is a free press and civil society able to criticise and monitor the actions of the government. The success of the Truth and Reconciliation Commission highlights the openness of South African society.

Arguments against

1   There is a fear that South Africa is becoming a one-party state. The ANC now controls all nine Provinces. Only in KwaZulu-Natal does it share power with the IFP. The NNP merged with the ANC in 2004. The ANC now has the power to change the Constitution and this could enable Mbeki to run for a third term. The ANC has 70% of Assembly seats. In contrast, the official opposition, the DA, has 12% of the seats.

2   There is an issue of corruption with leading ANC members such as Tony Yengeni being sent to jail. Former Deputy President Zuma's financial adviser was found guilty of corruption and Zuma was accused of being in a corrupt relationship with him. He was dismissed from office and was himself charged with corruption in 2006. The trial ended with Zuma's acquittal. Groups within the ANC have accused the Judiciary of being racist. (The majority of top judges are White.)

3   The federal system exists only on paper. Minority rights, such as Afrikaner and Zulu culture, are under threat. Mbeki appoints all nine Premiers of the Provinces and there is a lack of democracy within them.

4   Mbeki is intolerant of criticism. He accuses critics of being racists and has even attacked Archbishop Tutu. The policy of Transformation Politics could threaten the independence of judges and the rights of non-black South Africans. The South African Broadcasting Corporation (SABC) is regarded as being the mouthpiece of the ANC.

SOCIAL AND ECONOMIC ISSUES

The legacy of apartheid has created vast inequalities between the races in terms of income, ownership of the land and the economy, educational provision and attainment, and health. The one area where the legacy of apartheid is still strong is the distribution of land.

Policies and Progress in Education

- In 2004 the government invested 21% of the entire budget in education (6% of GNP)

- Progress has been made in reducing the number of schools with no sanitation, water or electricity. This number has been reduced to under 40% today.

- Black South Africans now make up more than 60% of students in higher education.

- Grade 12 matriculation results (equivalent to Scottish Highers) have improved significantly. In 1999 the pass rate was 48.9%; five years later it had risen to 70%.

Problems
- Substantial inequalities exist between the provinces. In the Western Cape, 96% of schools have electricity, whereas in the Eastern Cape, only 40% of schools have electricity.

- There is a massive skills shortage with industry finding it difficult to find staff, yet there are millions of unskilled, semi-literate unemployed workers.

- Schools in the poorest (black) communities suffer teacher shortages, overcrowding and buildings with no electricity or sanitation and only basic resources.

Land

Land Distribution: 62,000 out of 80,000 claims have been settled, yet black African ownership of land has only increased from 13% to 16%. Many black South Africans prefer financial compensation instead of being given land.

2005: The Constitutional Court confirmed the rights of white farmers against land invasion. The 'willing buyer–willing seller' principle will only be accepted if the farmer accepts a fair price. If this is rejected by the seller, the Constitution permits land to be expropriated.

September 2005: A landmark decision was taken to expropriate land from a white farmer, Hannes Vissar, who owned a 500 hectare farm in North West province. Vissar wanted R3 million but the government only offered R1.75 million.

In 2006 the Provincial Land Claims Commissioner said:
"Two-thirds of the country remains in the hands of less than 60,000 people, while 14 million black South Africans eke out a precarious existence in the former Homelands and urban informal settlements."

Housing

- The ANC's 1994 election promise to deliver one million new homes over a five-year period was unrealistic but was achieved over a ten-year period, although many of the new homes are starter homes rather than fully completed dwellings.

- Progress has been made in providing basic amenities such as electricity and running water. Privatisation of services has led to an increase in charges.

- Vast housing inequalities exist between the provinces and between the races. While 98% of households in the Western Cape have access to piped water, only 62% of households in the Eastern Cape have access.

- Racial segregation still exists. While the new rich black South African elite have moved into the former white areas with their swimming pools and servants, the majority of black South Africans still live in the former townships with limited facilities.

Health

▲ Significant progress has been made in improving primary health care. Provision of clean water to eight million black South Africans has been a key weapon against ill health and disease. Child mortality rates double when there is no access to clean water.

▲ Projects such as the National Primary School Nutrition for needy primary schoolchildren provide a 'Mandela sandwich' to more than five million children, increasing both educational achievement and attendance.

▲ A free health care programme for children under six and pregnant women has been implemented.

HIV/AIDS

South Africa faces an HIV/AIDS crisis. 4.5 million black South Africans suffer from HIV/AIDS and life expectancy has dropped from 62 years to 48 years.

The government of Thabo Mbeki was criticised for failing to give free anti-AIDS drugs to all HIV-positive pregnant women and their children. In October 2002 the government finally agreed to give out the drugs. Mbeki is not convinced that AIDS is caused by HIV.

Crime and the Law

The fear and impact of crime is one issue that unites all races. South Africa has one of the highest murder rates in the world and, on average, fifty five murders take place every day.

Government Action
▲ police budgets have been significantly increased, leading to a rise in the number of officers. With the new *Firearms Control Act* (2005) the government hopes to reduce the number of illegal guns which circulate in South Africa.

▲ the government claims that there has been a reduction in crime. However, the public does not share this perception that the streets are safer.

Employment: Black Economic Empowerment

Affirmative Action legislation has been passed to speed up the "transformation of South Africa's economic life".

The *Employment Equity Act* 1998 ensured that black South Africans receive preferential treatment in hiring, promotion, university admission and the awarding of government contracts.

Black Economic Empowerment Act (BEE) 2004

▲ Its purpose is to place more of the economy in black African hands by encouraging the growth of black African businesses and black African control of the stock exchange. The policy has created a wealthy black African elite who have become multi-millionaires, for example Cyril Ramaphosa (photo right) and Tokyo Sexwale.

▲ The policy has divided the black African community. The Trade Union Organisation (COSATU) argues that BEE helps only a "narrow group of individuals already rich," while the majority of black Africans live in poverty.

Achievements

▲ Almost 300,000 black Africans became middle income earners between 2002 and 2005

▲ The proportion of senior black African managers has increased from 37% to 55%

▲ Redistribution of income between the races has taken place

▲ The majority of the middle class are now black Africans

President Mbeki referred to South Africa as being a land of two nations—one White and rich, and one Black and poor. For a non-White living in a township with only basic amenities, a high crime rate, and poverty this statement is true. For the educated, prosperous black middle class the statement reflects the past as they live in their wealthy suburbs and drive their top-of-the-range cars—'Black Transformation' is a reality. South Africa is a country where the wealth gap between the white and, new, black elite and the poor, including unskilled Whites, is widening.

Study Theme 3B:
The People's Republic of China

Reference to the Pulse Publications textbook *Studies in International Relations* (Second edition), China, Chapters 14–18 and www.modernityscotland.com will enhance the use of these revision notes. It is assumed that you have studied the course and have a sound understanding of the key political, social and economic issues facing China.

EXAM REQUIREMENTS

You are expected to display knowledge and understanding of:

1 The Chinese political system: the role and powers of the Chinese government at national, regional, and local levels.

2 Political Issues: participation and representation; the role of the Communist Party of China and the extent of political opposition; political trends.

3 Social and Economic Issues: the nature and extent of social and economic inequalities and change; the effectiveness of government responses and the consequences for different groups.

KEY FEATURES OF CHINA

China is the third largest country in the world by area and its 1.3 billion citizens make it the most populated country in the world.

China is a Communist country with its ideology based on the teachings of Marx, Lenin and Mao. Chairman Mao established Communism in China in 1949 and ruled by dictatorship until his death in 1976.

China is an emerging superpower and is a permanent member of the UN Security Council. It has a large standing army and has nuclear weapons.

China has the fastest growing economy in the world and is becoming an industrial giant. This is creating significant environmental and social pressures.

China has managed to introduce 'capitalist' changes to its economy without introducing political change. The Communist Party of Chins (CPC) has loosened economic and social controls in the country, while retaining total political control. Dissent is not tolerated and China has a poor human rights record.

The present Chinese leader is Hu Jintao (photo right) who replaced Jiang Zemin. Both leaders have continued the economic reforms of Deng Xiaoping who ruled China from 1978 until his death in 1997. While Mao's slogan was 'Serve the people', Deng's was 'To get rich is glorious'.

Key issue:
The transformation of a state-controlled economic system to a market economy.

CHINA'S ECONOMY

Deng Xiaoping dismantled the commune system in the countryside and introduced the household responsibility system which allowed peasants to produce food for private sale. The creation of Special Economic Zones (SEZs) enabled China to accept foreign capital and adopt foreign technologies.

The inefficient and heavily subsidised state-owned factories were opened to market forces. This caused many to close and led to unemployment. Under the subsidised system of the 'iron rice bowl', Chinese workers were guaranteed jobs and houses for life, but now this system has ended.

The economy of China is the second largest in the world based on its Gross Domestic Product (GDP). However, China's huge population of 1.3 billion results in a relatively low per capita income.

China's GDP rose from just under 600 billion yuan in 1996 to 4,500 billion yuan in 2005.

Key issue:
To what extent have economic reforms improved the living standards of the people?

China's economy is booming and many people are becoming rich and buying consumer items that their parents could only dream about. China, for example, has the fastest growing vehicle market in the world.

Prosperity has created a significant number of yuan millionaires and billionaires.

Special Economic Zones (SEZs), which are based around China's coastal cities and regions, have contributed to China's new wealth. China's exports have doubled over the last five years.

However, the economic boom has widened inequalities between town and countryside and between regions in China. The ending of an 'iron rice bowl' has created poverty and unemployment for many Chinese citizens. A booming economy has fuelled inflation and brought hardship to those on a low income.

In 2002 the disposable income for rural dwellers was a modest $290; for urban dwellers it was $964—over three times more.

Living standards in the countryside are improving but not at the same rate as in the towns. Township enterprises have been set up in rural areas to encourage enterprise activities.

At the 2006 National People's Congress Prime Minister Wen Jiabao restated that the government's priority was to bring about rapid and significant change in rural areas which, he admitted, had lagged far behind the booming urban areas. The creation of the 'new socialist countryside' would be brought about by the new Five-Year Plan which is based on a modest prediction of 7.5% annual growth, on average, through to 2010.

The government outlined the following reforms:
- agricultural tax to be abolished in 2006
- an experimental health care insurance scheme to be extended to cover 40% of counties
- tuition and other fees for rural students receiving compulsory education to be eliminated by the end of 2007.
- central government spending on rural areas for all services ranging from health care to subsidies for grain producers to be increased by 14.2% in 2006–2007
- government spending on infrastructure will be shifted towards rural areas. This will lead to new roads, water and power supplies, schools and hospitals. These projects will create employment and improve life in the countryside.

However, critics argue that these reforms are modest and depend on the ability of local government to contribute financially. The extra money spent will only raise central government spending on the countryside to 8.9% of total government expenditure. (This is up from 2005's 8.8%, but down from the 9.2% spent in 2004.) Also, while the government promises to compensate local government for the abolition of school fees through spending an extra 218 billion yuan on rural schools over the next five years, there is no guarantee that this will cover all the financial shortfalls.

Those living in the countryside have lower incomes and have access to fewer services.

Furthermore the reforms do not deal with the farmers' inability to defend their land against developers. (Many do not have clear legal rights to their fields.) It is estimated that some 200 million rural Chinese people have little or no work. The government has no intention of allowing them to migrate to the urban areas. The new Five-Year Plan predicts only a modest increase in officially allowed migrant numbers from an annual average of eight million.

Economic migrants are a major problem (see The Houku) and suffer significant inequalities. State benefits for the unemployed are limited in China and with the closure of many state-owned enterprises, unemployment has become a major issue.

The Hukou

The Hukou links every Chinese citizen to a home district, outside which they have few rights to welfare benefits, medical care or schooling. The Chinese government has announced it will gradually abolish the system. However, it is worried that a massive invasion from the rural and poor regions of China to the wealthier cities will take place. In November 2005, eleven provinces along the developed eastern coast, which needs an influx of labour, were allowed to abolish the Hukou.

Those who do move to the cities without permission are regarded as illegal immigrant workers. It is estimated that this 'floating population' of immigrants numbers about 100 million. They are exploited by unscrupulous managers and forced to work long hours for low pay. They cannot complain as they have no legal rights.

Migrant workers have no rights. What are the consequences for this young family?

Key issue:
To what extent have economic reforms created environmental and social problems?

SOCIAL AND ENVIRONMENTAL ISSUES IN CHINA

China's economic growth is taking a heavy toll on the environment and public health. China's towns and countryside are experiencing smog, water shortages, soil erosion and acid rain.

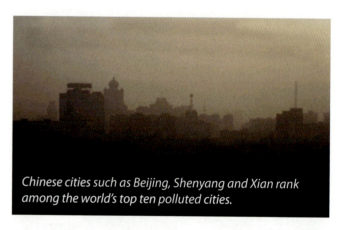

Chinese cities such as Beijing, Shenyang and Xian rank among the world's top ten polluted cities.

■ Health inequalities, especially between urban and rural communities, are widening. Many patients cannot afford the medical costs of going to a doctor or a hospital.

■ Despite China's significant economic growth, unemployment is increasing. China's entry to the World Trade Organisation and the collapse of many state-owned enterprises (SOEs) will further fuel unemployment. The inefficiency of SOEs often meant that goods were worth less than the cost of making them.

■ State benefits for the unemployed are limited. Over the past decade more than a million people have lost their jobs in Shanghai.

■ China's public education system is facing a crisis. Local government is expected to pay most of the cost of education but is failing to do so. Although education is supposed to be free, parents are expected to contribute to their child's education to a greater or lesser degree depending on where they live.

Schools have been encouraged to go into business to produce consumer goods or to rent out school rooms to enterprises, some of which are illegal.

POLITICAL CONTROL IN CHINA

An assessment of China's record on Human Rights

China functions as a one-party state in which all aspects of social, economic and political life are dominated by the Communist Party. While the Constitution guarantees "the fundamental rights of every citizen", these rights must be exercised to support the Chinese socialist system.

The structure of the Communist Party of China ensures tight control from the top through 'democratic centralism'. The National Congress, for example, only meets once every five years and announces the Party's policies for the next few years. Membership of the powerful Standing Committee of the Politbureau is decided behind the scenes at Congress. The government structure largely duplicates that of the CPC. The present leader, President Hu, heads all three branches of power—party, state and military.

● Membership of the CPC is limited and stands at about 66 million (5% of the population). Membership is by invitation and even capitalists can join the Party. Corruption and nepotism are major criticisms made against the Party.

● All demands for political reform have been discouraged and crushed. The Chinese Democracy Movement demanded the introduction of democracy. Its founding document was a magazine article entitled *The Fifth Modernisation* which was published in the late 1970s.

The National People's Congress is China's parliament but it is just a rubber stamp for the leadership's decisions.

The Democracy Movement has never recovered from the brutal massacre of 2,000 democracy supporters in Tiananmen Square in 1989. Open opposition to the government is a rare occurrence in China and when it does take place a brutal crackdown results. In 1998,

for example, the China Democracy Party was created. The new party demanded freedom of speech, a new constitution and free elections. The party was immediately declared illegal and its leaders arrested and jailed.

● Citizens are expected to participate through their official trade union (controlled by the CPC) and through their urban residents' committee. In the countryside, the 930,000 villages in China are allowed to elect their own village committees. The Party screens all candidates and only 40% of those elected are not Party members.

● In recent years the number of labour disputes and protests involving massive numbers of workers has risen dramatically. Workers have been protesting about conditions of employment, low wages and corrupt management. Independent trade unions are not permitted in China and any action by workers outwith the official All China Federation of Trade Unions (ACFTU) is illegal.

Since the 1990s the rapid growth of private, including foreign, enterprise and the widespread closure of state-owned industries has reduced trade union membership and Party control at the grassroots. By 1999 trade union membership had fallen to 87 million, down from over 100 million in 1990. An official 2004 survey found that trade unions had been established in only 10% of the 500,000 foreign enterprises registered in China. The Communist

Party is now taking action to restore its control over the factory floor. It argues that it is protecting the rights of the workers by demanding that trade unions be set up in privately run enterprises. In 2006 the American company Wal-Mart reluctantly allowed its 31,000 Chinese workforce to form trade unions.

The limitations placed on democratic rule in Hong Kong are clear evidence that the Chinese government has no intention of relaxing its political dictatorship. Only half of the delegates on Hong Kong's legislative council are directly elected; the other half are appointed by the Chinese leadership. Nevertheless, the people of Hong Kong have political and religious rights not enjoyed by their fellow Chinese citizens. Religious freedom and criticism of the government are permitted. Groups such as Falun Gong and the Chinese Democracy Movement are not illegal and protest marches are permitted. In 2004, ten thousand people took to the streets of Hong Kong to protest against Bejing's ruling that it alone will determine the shape and timing of elections in the city.

The media is tightly controlled by the government with many of the largest media organisations, namely CCTV, *The People's Daily* and Xinhua, being agencies of the Chinese government.

Recently there has been some relaxation with some open discussion of social issues. Access to the Internet is heavily restricted. All of the 100,000 Internet cafes are required to use software that controls what website users can see. Amnesty International has criticised Google for agreeing to restrict the information it provides in China effectively allowing the Chinese government to censor information.

China's Human Rights Record

The lack of political rights and the arrest of dissidents are abuses of human rights. China's policy towards ethnic minorities under its rule has been to encourage Chinese people to migrate to areas such as Tibet, Mongolia and Xinjiang. In Xinjiang, the Uighurs now make up less than half of the population. Minority groups claim that the Chinese are destroying their culture and any protests are crushed by the Chinese military.

The Chinese government claims that legislation passed in 2005 provides legal protection for religious believers and safeguards religious freedom in China. However, this only applies to recognised religions. Of the more than 200 million religious believers in China, only about 140 million belong to registered religious groups. The Vatican does not recognise the 'patriotic Catholic Church in China' and the Chinese authorities do not allow the Pope to appoint bishops. All those religious believers who do not belong to the Patriotic Religious Associations face persecution from the Chinese government.

It is not only religious groups which suffer. Falun Gong, a Chinese Qigong practice which is supposed to improve the mind, body and spirit, has been classified as an evil cult and has been banned. It now operates underground.

In August 2006 *Time* magazine reported the destruction of a church and an attack on its parishioners by the security police. The attack happened in the suburbs of Hangzhou, a city 180 km south of Shanghai. The Christians had failed to register with the authorities and as such their Church and their service were illegal.

The one-child policy has been one of the most unpopular policies in China, especially in the countryside. The State Family Planning Commission sets the national birth rate and provincial quotas. It is still common for overzealous officials to insist that women undergo 'forced abortions'.

In 2005 Chen Guangcheng (opposite), a blind legal activist, highlighted the forced sterilisation measures used by local officials in Shandong province. Chen hoped that higher level officials would step in and stop this illegal practice which featured in an article in *Time* magazine. Instead Chen was arrested and in September 2006, after a two-hour trial, he was sentenced to more than four years in prison.

The government claims that the one-child policy has made the nation prosperous and has enabled China to solve the problem of how to feed a population of 1.3 billion people. One consequence of the policy is that China's population is rapidly ageing. By 2050, the over-65s will make up over 23% of the population as opposed to 7% in 2000.

China's legal and prison system has been heavily criticised. The death penalty is still used and it is estimated that about 10,000 people are executed each year. (The number of people executed in China is regarded as a state secret.) Amnesty International has also accused the Chinese authorities of selling organs taken from executed prisoners.

The Laogai is the name given to the network of prisons, labour camps and 'hospitals' which exist in China. The Laogai is based on two principles: hard labour and political thought reform. In China all prisoners are forced to work, often in highly unsafe conditions. Individuals can be held for up to three years with no trial or sentencing procedures in Re-education (Laojiao) Camps.

Less than a minute after raising their banner in Tiananmen Square, these Western Falun Gong practitioners were surrounded by police. Within ten minutes they had all been rounded up and whisked away to jail. "Why did you arrest us? What law did we break?" a woman asked. The policeman replied, "Those three words, 'Truth, Compassion, Tolerance', are illegal in China."

Study Theme 3C
The United States of America

Reference to the Pulse Publications textbook *Studies in International Relations* (Second edition), United States of America, Chapters 4–8 and www.modernityscotland.com will enhance the use of these revision notes. It is assumed that you have studied the course and have a sound understanding of the key political, social and economic issues facing the USA.

EXAM REQUIREMENTS

You are expected to display knowledge and understanding of:

1   The US political system: the role and powers of the US government at federal, state and local level.

2   Political Issues: participation and representation; immigration. political parties and support from different groups; political trends.

3   Social and Economic Issues: (case study: ethnic minorities) the nature and extent of social and economic inequalities; demand for change; the effectiveness of government responses and the consequences for different groups.

BACKGROUND

The USA is the fourth largest country in the world in area and has a population of 284 million. It is the home of capitalism and its companies and products are to be found across the globe. Whites make up 70% of the population. Hispanics, at 13%, have overtaken Blacks as the second largest group. Blacks make up 12% of the population.

The largest Hispanic group is Mexican Americans (66%). They are attracted to the USA by its high living standards and accept low paid work such as labouring in the fields or working as servants. There are many illegal aliens from Mexico in the USA where immigration is a major issue. Other Hispanic groups are Puerto Rican, Cuban and those from Central and South America.

The majority of the Blacks (54%) live in the South for historical reasons. Outside the South, Blacks overwhelmingly live in the metropolitan areas of the North and West. Within these cities, 70% of Blacks live in the ghettos.

Key issue:
To what extent do Congress and the Supreme Court limit the power of the President?

THE SYSTEM OF GOVERNMENT IN THE USA

The USA has a federal system of government where power is divided between the central (Federal) government and the fifty states such as Florida. The power of the Federal government is balanced against the rights of the state governments and the people. All powers not assigned by the Constitution to the Federal government are reserved for the states.

The Constitution defines the respective powers and duties of the Executive (President), legislature (Congress) and Judiciary (Supreme Court). This is referred to as the separation of powers.

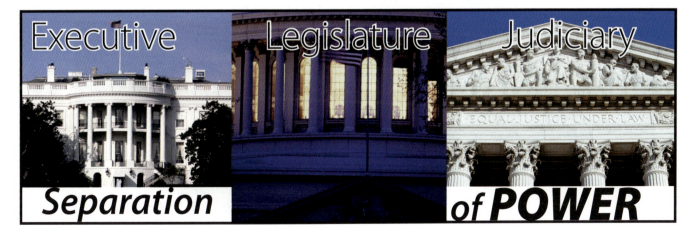

For a law to be made it has to be passed by both the Senate and the House of Representatives and finally be signed by the President. It does not become law if the President uses his veto. In July 2006 Bush used his first veto to oppose a Bill to fund stem cell research.

The power of the President is checked by both Congress and the Supreme Court. Congress can overturn a veto if it has a two-thirds majority in both Houses and while the President draws up the budget each year, Congress has to vote through the money. The President can make foreign treaties but again two-thirds of the Senate must agree.

The nine members of the Supreme Court can declare a law or the actions of a President to be unconstitutional. Also, they can change the way existing laws are applied by redefining what they mean. The nine Supreme Court Judges are appointed for life by the President. The death of one judge and the retirement of another enabled Bush to make new appointments which had to be ratified by the Senate.

The election system also checks the power of the President. He or she can only be elected for two terms (a maximum of eight years). Members of the House of Representatives are elected every two years and Senators for six years. This means that the President can face a hostile Congress. President Clinton, a Democrat, faced a Republican Congress. In contrast, President Bush's party, the Republicans, controlled Congress up till the elections in November 2006, when the Democrats took control of both Houses.

President Bush – the Imperial President?

President Clinton was described as 'the defensive President' who faced a hostile Republican-dominated Congress. In contrast Bush was referred to as 'the Imperial President'. Up till November 2006 his own party controlled both the House and the Senate. This, along with the 'war against terrorism' has allowed Bush to expand the office of the Presidency.

The terrorist attack on the Twin Towers in September 2001 increased the powers of President Bush. As Commander-in-Chief of the armed forces he has passed legislation and created structures which have strengthened the Executive. The *USA PATRIOT Act* gives the Attorney General the power to order the detention of anyone whom s/he has "reasonable grounds" to suspect is "a terrorist". With an Executive order issued in 2001, the President gave the Attorney General the power to overrule the courts if they ordered the release of someone deemed to be a terrorist. In July 2006 the Supreme Court ruled that the special military tribunals set up to try suspected foreign terrorists in Guantanamo Bay were unlawful. The Supreme Court set limits on the President's claim that, as Commander-in-Chief he can do what he wishes to protect the American people in time of war. The Supreme Court reaffirmed its

President George W Bush

authority to preserve the constitutional safeguards of civil liberties, even in wartime.

Mid-term elections 2006

The 2006 results ended any further debate about Bush being an 'Imperial President'. The election was a disaster for the Republican Party, which lost control of both the House of Representatives (which was expected) and the Senate (which was unexpected). In the elections for State Governors, the Democrats also made gains, taking control of six more states, thus bringing their total number of Governors up to twenty eight, with the Republicans on twenty two.

In the House of Representatives, the Democrats won 234 seats to the Republicans' 201, almost an exact reversal of the Republicans' pre-election majority. The new Speaker of the House of Representatives, Nancy Pelosi, is the first woman to hold this office. She has

Nancy Pelosi has promised to lead "the most honest, most open and most ethical Congress in history".

promised to lead "the most honest, most open and most ethical Congress in history". The Democrats now control the Senate by a narrow margin. While the Democrats and the Republicans each have forty nine seats, the two Independent Senators, Joe Lieberman and Bernie Sanders, are anti-Republican.

In exit polls three-quarters of voters said that corruption in government affected their vote with 60% saying they opposed the war in Iraq. Significantly Donald Rumsfeld, the Defence Secretary and architect of the invasion of Iraq, resigned and was replaced by the more pragmatic Robert Gates.

The election results have greatly weakened President Bush, especially in domestic affairs. He will now have to compromise with the Democratic majority and he will certainly make greater use of his power of veto. It will be difficult, for example, for President Bush to get his 2001 tax cuts renewed as the Democrats regard them as a handout for the rich.

2006 ELECTION RESULTS

House of Representatives

	2000	2004	2006
Democrats	212	202	234
Republicans	221	232	201
Independents	2	1	-

Senate

	2000	2004	2006
Democrats	50	44	49
Republicans	50	55	49
Independents	0	1	2

Key issue:
To what extent do race, gender, income, and religion influence voting behaviour?

POLITICAL PARTIES AND THEIR SUPPORT

Unlike their British counterparts, political parties in the USA have no national party structure and exist as a national entity only when they choose their presidential candidate at the National Convention held every four years.

The two major political parties in the USA are the Republican Party and the Democratic Party.

Republicans

Party of big business; support concentrated in the Midwest and the South in more rural and suburban areas; more middle and higher income earners support them; support from people with conservative views including the religious right.

Democrats

Support concentrated in coastal areas and major cities; traditionally get support from blue-collar manual workers, ethnic minority groups and poorer people; support comes from people with liberal viewpoints.

CHANGING POLITICAL SUPPORT

Gender

Traditionally, women have been more likely to vote Democrat. However, the Republicans have been making inroads into this vote and in the 2004 Presidential election the Democrats had a narrow majority of 51% of women voters compared to 48% for the Republicans. When one looks at the White-only vote, though, a different picture emerges. White women voted 55% to 44% in favour of the Republicans (White men 62% to 37% in favour of the Republicans).

Race

As indicated above, race and ethnicity is an important factor in party support in the USA. The black vote overwhelmingly goes to the Democrats. In the 2004 election the Democrats won 89% of the black vote. The Republicans increased their support from 9% to 11% which reflects their attempt to win over middle-class Christian Blacks under the age of 35. A similar strategy has paid dividends with Hispanic voters and in 2004 the Republicans won 45% of the Hispanic vote reducing the Democrats' share to 55%.

ELECTING THE PRESIDENT OF THE USA

The system for the election of the President of the USA requires a candidate to win the most votes in the electoral college. The candidate who wins the most votes in a state (the popular vote) gets all the electoral college votes from that state. California, the state with the most people, has fifty four electoral college votes while small states such as Montana have only three electoral college votes. This explains why Al Gore did not win the 2000 Presidential election despite receiving 500,000 more votes than George Bush. Although George Bush lost the popular vote, he won a narrow majority of the electoral college votes and so became the President.

In the 2004 Presidential election Bush was re-elected as President with a clear victory in both the popular vote and the electoral college. Bush increased the number of votes he received from 50 million to al-

most 60 million, showing how popular he was with the American people.

Critics have pointed out that there is still a clear race divide and that Bush failed to win over the African/American and Hispanic voters. There are no black Republican members of Congress. In contrast there are thirty seven black Democrat representatives in Congress. Bush has made progress in winning greater Hispanic support. There are four Hispanic Republicans in Congress compared to eighteen Hispanic Democrats. Wealthy Hispanics, especially the Cubans, identify with the Republican Party.

TO WHAT EXTENT HAVE ETHNIC MINORITIES MADE POLITICAL PROGRESS IN THE USA?

Points for

1 There was an increase in Black representation at Federal level in the House of Representatives from twenty five in 1991 to forty two in 2004 with a modest one in the Senate.

   Hispanic representation in the House of Representatives increased from eleven in 1991 to twenty four in 2004 and for the first time there are now two Hispanic Senators.

2 While black voter turnout is still low, Hispanic turnout is increasing. In 2000 just over 6 million Hispanics voted, but in 2004, 9.3 million turned out, an increase of 50% in four years.

3 The Black Caucus (the vast majority are Democrats) work as a group to increase their influence over issues of interest to African Americans. Furthermore, several Blacks have seniority in Congress and are chairpersons of powerful Congressional Committees. The Democratic Party depends on the Black vote.

4 Minorities are represented in Bush's Cabinet. Condoleeza Rice became Secretary of State in 2005 (Colin Powell had become the first black American to hold the post of Secretary of State in Bush's first administration). Alberto Gonzales is the Attorney General.

Points against

1 Blacks are still under-represented in Congress. In proportion to their population size there should be fifty three black Congressmen/women and twelve black Senators.

   Hispanics are still under-represented in Congress. In proportion to their population size there should be fifty six Hispanic Congressmen/women and thirteen Hispanic Senators.

2 The Hispanic population is increasing rapidly so voter turnout should increase. Hispanic turnout is still only 47% compared to Blacks at 56% and 68% for Whites.

3 The close political links between Blacks and the Democrats can be counterproductive if the Democrats are not in power. Up till the election of November 2006, the Presidency, the House of Representatives and the Senate were all controlled by the Republicans.

4 There is still a lack of role models for ethnic minorities. Neither the Democratic nor Republican Parties has had a member of an ethnic minority as its candidate for President or vice-President.

WHY IS BLACK AND HISPANIC ELECTION TURNOUT LOW?

1   Many Blacks and Hispanics suffer from apathy and alienation. They believe there is little point in voting as it will not change anything—they will remain in poverty.

2   The higher their level of education, the more likely a person is to vote. A higher proportion of Blacks and Hispanics than Whites drop out of high school and higher education. A significant number of Hispanics do not speak English or have only basic literacy.

3   Many have no interest in politics and politicians and do not register to vote. As such even if they decided to vote on the day, they would not be able to do so.

SOCIAL AND ECONOMIC INEQUALITY IN THE BLACK AND HISPANIC COMMUNITIES

Economic Inequalities
- Income levels including welfare
- Unemployment rates
- Promotion

Social Inequalities
- Housing
- Family structures
- Education
- Health
- Crime

Statistics of Poverty
- Three times as many Blacks (14.6%) as Whites (4.4%) earn less than $10,000 a year
- Unemployment among Blacks is over 10% and is double the figure for Whites
- Blacks are more likely to drop out of school and to enter the workforce with no qualifications
- In a country where health has to be paid for, one in four Blacks have no health insurance compared to one in ten Whites
- Life expectancy for Blacks is 72 years, while for Whites it is 77 years
- Although they make up only 12% of the population, 47% of all jail inmates are black and 55% of prisoners sentenced to death are black

The American Dream, whereby hard work and self-help can enable American citizens to move from poverty to prosperity and success, is not the American reality for many ethnic minorities. The USA is a very unequal society and millions of Americans live in poverty.

Poverty in the Black community

Black families who live in the ghetto are victims of the poverty cycle. Being born poor generally leads to a poor education, a low paid job or unemployment, and poverty which in turn leads to the children of these people being born poor.

Black Family Life

The 30% who form the black middle class live in the traditional family with two parents looking after the children. In the ghetto over 80% of black families are single parent families, headed in most cases by a woman.

The ghetto lifestyle of poor education, unemployment, substance abuse and crime has created a dependency culture. There is no male role model for young black boys who show no respect to their mothers.

Welfare payments in America have also been reduced with the number of individuals receiving food stamps decreasing. In 1996 the figure stood at 26 million; by 2001 it was less than 18 million.

Poverty in the Hispanic Community

The barrio is the Hispanic equivalent of the ghetto and here many Hispanics live in poverty, facing unemployment, limited education and poor health. Hispanics are over three times more likely to be poor when compared to Whites, but only marginally less likely to be poor compared to Blacks.

Poverty is not evenly distributed throughout the Hispanic subgroups. Puerto Ricans and Mexican Americans are more likely to suffer from poverty than Cubans. Many Hispanics have become middle class by starting their own businesses. Miami, in Florida, is where a significant number of Cubans have settled and the city has become a centre for finance and banking through its commerce links with South America. Cuban educational attainment is closer to that of Whites, with 23% of Cubans being college graduates compared to 26% of Whites but only 7% of Mexican Americans.

Unemployment

Hispanic unemployment is higher than that for Whites but lower than that for Blacks. Cuban unemployment rates are lower than those for the other Hispanic groups because fewer of them are recent immigrants. The overall unemployment rate for Hispanics is 7.5% with the rate for Puerto Ricans being 9.4% and Cubans 6.7%.

Family lifestyles and crime

The family is more central to life in the Hispanic community, especially among Cubans, than in the black underclass. While 69% of Black births are to unmarried mothers, the figure for Hispanics is 41%.

Hispanics are more likely to be the victims of crime than Whites but less likely than Blacks. Furthermore, the proportion of the Hispanic population in jail is three times higher than the proportion of Whites who are in jail.

Asians

They are the success story with many having achieved the American Dream. Asians have become very successful in the business world and in education and are noted for their drive and ambition.

Statistics of Success

- 35% of Asians have incomes of more than $75,000, compared to 27% of Whites and 16% of Blacks

- 44% of Asians are college graduates compared to 26% of Whites

TO WHAT EXTENT HAVE SOCIAL AND ECONOMIC INEQUALITIES BEEN REDUCED?

There are essentially two black communities. Middle-class Blacks have lived the American Dream and have experienced significant improvements in their living standards. Blacks who have remained in the ghetto suffer from poverty, high unemployment rates, high crime rates and drug abuse. Over 80% of black families in the ghetto are lone parent families

- Poverty levels for Blacks and Hispanics have decreased over the last seventeen years.

In 1991 almost a third of Blacks (31.9%) experienced poverty; now the figure stands at 22%. Hispanic poverty in the same period decreased from 28% to 21%. However, there is still a massive gap between the races with fewer than 8% of Whites living in poverty. Only 10% of Asian and Pacific Islanders (API), who make up 4% of the population, live in poverty.

What is affirmative action?

Affirmative action was a series of programmes and measures designed to overcome discrimination in employment and education.

- Quotas were set for organisations such as the police and the fire brigade to employ a certain number of ethnic minority workers.

- At colleges and universities preference was given to minority candidates, for example to enter medicine and law. They were allowed entry with inferior qualifications to counterbalance the poor quality of education they might have received.

- In employment, companies who wanted contracts from the federal or state government had to introduce affirmative action programmes in the hiring and promotion of workers.

- Busing was a very controversial form of affirmative action. It describes a series of programmes to transport children across towns in order to create a greater race balance in schools. White parents were angry that their children would have to leave a wealthy school in the suburbs to travel to a run-down inner city school. A 1995 Supreme Court decision effectively ended busing.

SHOULD AFFIRMATIVE ACTION CONTINUE?

Arguments for ending Affirmative Action

1 President Bush described affirmative action as "quota systems that … exclude people from higher education … (and) are divisive, unfair and impossible to square with the Constitution".

2 Affirmative action created a dependency culture in the black community. It did not encourage black people to develop a culture of enterprise.

3 Affirmative action was not a success; Blacks and Hispanics are still not equal to Whites. The USA is still not a tolerant society. Many Whites resent being the victims of reverse discrimination.

Arguments for continuing Affirmative Action

1 President Clinton argued that the job of ending discrimination remained unfinished and strongly defended affirmative action: "Mend it don't end it!"

2 Ethnic minorities have made great advances due to affirmative action which has helped to create a black middle class who have achieved the American Dream.

3 Affirmative action was a success and its ending has had a negative impact on the social and economic advancement of ethnic minorities. The University of California, when banned from using affirmative action for admissions, suffered a 40% decline in minority admissions.

Affirmative Action

In a Persistent Vegetative State

US IMMIGRATION DEBATE

Illegal immigration is a deeply divisive issue in the United States and was an important topic during the November 2006 mid-term elections

Why is it an issue?

Polls indicate that a majority of Americans see illegal immigrants as serious problem. There are an estimated 11.5 million illegal immigrants in the United States. Many of these people are poorly educated, unskilled workers who occupy the sort of jobs most American citizens would not take—at least not at the same low salary. The business lobby sees immigrants as beneficial to the USA; the social conservative lobby regards them as detrimental. Congress, at present, is trying to draw up a Bill which is acceptable to both sides. At the state level Georgia has passed a law, which will take effect in July 2007, preventing illegal immigrants from receiving state benefits.

Political Issues

Following the destruction of the World Trade Centre in September 2001, attitudes have hardened towards illegal immigrants. Congress has passed two Acts – the *USA PATRIOT Act* and the *Border Security Act* which restrict and control the entry of aliens to the USA.

Study Theme 3E:
The Politics of Development in Africa

(with the exception of the Republic of South Africa)

Reference to the Pulse Publications' textbook *Studies in International Relations*, chapters 1-3 and www. modernityscotland.com will enhance the use of these revision notes. It is assumed that you have studied the course and have a sound understanding of the key political, social and economic factors affecting development in Africa.

EXAM REQUIREMENTS

You are expected to display knowledge and understanding of:

1   Health and health care issues: access to education, food and safe water. The link between health, education, food and development.

2   Economic, political and social factors affecting development.

3   Roles and effectiveness of: African Governments; African Union; NGOs; UK; EU; UN in promoting development.

Key issue:
To what extent do economic, political and social factors affect development?

ECONOMIC FACTORS

Debt

Many African governments have borrowed money to finance development. The conditions which are normally attached to these loans have led to extreme hardships for the countries involved. For example, the IMF can insist that education and health programmes are cut to reduce government spending in order to keep up repayments. On the other hand, if used effectively, debt cancellation can promote development. In April 2006 the government of Zambia was able to introduce free health care for people living in rural areas, scrapping fees that for years had made health care inaccessible for millions. This move has been made possible as a direct result of the government using the money from debt cancellation and aid increases. These were agreed at the G8 Summit in Gleneagles in July 2005 when Zambia received $4 billion of debt relief to invest in health and education.

Heavily Indebted Poor Countries (HIPC) Initiative

This was launched in 1996 to provide HIPC countries with relief from debt. However, the qualifying conditions are difficult to achieve and in 2005 only around 10% of the debt owed by HIPC countries had been cancelled. The UK government has cancelled 100% of the debt owed to it by HIPC countries.

Cash Crops

Cash crops are those grown for sale on the open market for profit and not domestic consumption. They are usually grown to satisfy the requirements of receiving a loan from the IMF, but also to earn money from export sales in order to repay debts. This can generate much-needed income but it can cause problems for small farmers who have to rely on one commodity, especially if the world price for the crop falls or, even worse, if the crop fails. It also reduces the land available for growing food for local consumption. In Burkino Faso growing peanuts for sale is tempting to poor farmers as a means to make money. However, this cash crop needs more water more often, requires artificial fertilisers to maintain soil fertility and reduces the land available for grazing. In years of low yield farmers can end up in debt and in prosperous years, as more and more

Cash crops may require more water

farmers plant cash crops, the price can fall which again leads to debts. Furthermore, the soil quickly becomes exhausted.

Terms of Trade

There is a view that free trade not free aid is the most effective way to promote development. For instance, it is estimated that for every £1 given in aid to African countries £2 is taken back due to unfair terms of trade. The insistence on free markets by the WTO can make it difficult for African producers to compete on equal terms in world markets. While subsidies are withheld from African producers, EU farmers are subsidised through the CAP. Likewise, import taxes are not permitted in case they inhibit free and equal trade, whereas foreign surplus produce is dumped in African countries and sold more cheaply than local produce. This seriously disadvantages African producers.

In 2004, Tate and Lyle, a multinational sugar company, received around £120 million from the CAP. This was mostly in the form of export subsidies which, according to Oxfam, led to surpluses on the world market. These in turn undercut local producers, and put them out of business in Ethiopia, Mozambique and Malawi.

TO WHAT EXTENT DO POLITICAL FACTORS AFFECT DEVELOPMENT?

Armed Conflict

Armed conflict ultimately leads to food shortages. It can destroy a country's infrastructure making it difficult to distribute food supplies and aid thereby hampering any prospect of economic and social development. In a war situation governments can divert food supplies and money to feed their soldiers or pay for their own military needs. They can also employ scorched earth policies and contaminate water supplies and wells as a means of depriving their enemies of food and water. This invariably leads to refugees who become non-productive and aid dependent. This situation is often made worse if emergency aid is suspended or stopped in order to safeguard aid workers.

Refugees are often the result of armed conflict as people are forced from their homes.

Bad Governance and Kleptocracy

Bad governance is a key issue in explaining lack of development in many African countries. Money is either wasted by bad governance or diverted by corrupt or kleptocratic governments away from social services to pay for weapons and the military and to shore up corrupt political systems. This can also lead to the temporary suspension of aid until donor countries believe that it will be used efficiently and effectively by governments to promote development. According to the *New York Times* in May 2006, bad governance in Zimbabwe has created enormous economic problems. The annual inflation rate is currently around 1,200% (the highest in the world). Shortages of foreign currency to pay for fuel, food and other commodities, along with 70% unemployment have accelerated the economic meltdown. It is also the country hardest hit by the brain drain in Africa, resulting in a loss of 50% of key professionals within the public health institutions.

TO WHAT EXTENT DO SOCIAL FACTORS AFFECT DEVELOPMENT?

Health

HIV/AIDS has reached epidemic status and is one of the biggest challenges to development in Africa today. The resultant pressure and demands placed upon the provision of health care are proving too much to cope with, causing major social problems. The economy is also suffering, with rising HIV/AIDS rates being linked to falls in GDP since the majority of those infected with HIV/AIDS are of working age meaning that key workers and professionals who are essential for development are becoming too ill to work or are dying. Africa has already lost seven million farmers to AIDS and it is estimated that by 2020, the disease will have claimed a further 20% of southern Africa's farmworkers. In Zimbabwe, 25% of the population is infected with HIV and 40% of all deaths are AIDS-related.

Malaria is the major cause of death in Africa today. The consequences for development are similar to those for HIV/AIDS and together they are proving to be catastrophic for the economy since the high mortality rate reduces the productive workforce, leaving employers, schools, factories and hospitals constantly having to find and train new staff from a reduced workforce. 95% of all malaria cases are in Africa where an African child dies every 30 seconds as a result of malaria.

Farming Methods

Inefficient farming methods such as deforestation, overcropping and overgrazing are exhausting the land in many African countries. Also, erosion, salination or desertification, along with poor irrigation and water management, are reducing available fertile farmland. Ethiopia's poverty-stricken economy is based on agriculture and accounts for half of its GDP, 60% of exports and 80% of total employment. However, this sector suffers from poor farming methods and cultivation practices—deforestation, overgrazing, soil erosion and water shortages in some areas due to water-intensive farming methods and poor management.

Land Tenure and Women

Traditionally, women are excluded from the right to own or inherit land and from agricultural training and information. They are often only given poor or marginal land despite them doing the most agricultural work. This presents a serious problem for development since women generally have the responsibility for producing food for consumption while men are usually involved in the production of cash crops for export. According to the UN,

In Ghana women make up 52% of the agricultural workforce, produce 70% of subsistence crops, but are denied full land rights.

women do 66% of the work in the world and produce 50% of the food, yet earn only 5% of the income and own less than 1% of the world's property.

Education

There is no free education for many children in Africa (89 out of 103 developing countries charge school fees) and as a result attendance at primary school, especially for girls, is very low. When school fees were abolished in Uganda, Tanzania, and Kenya, 7 million additional children, many of them girls, started school. This situation is affecting the numbers of future professionals needed to assist development. According to the UN, 66% of children denied primary education are girls and 75% of the world's 876 million illiterate adults are women. Also, every extra year a girl spends at school could reduce child mortality by 10%. Two of the UN Millennium Development Goals (MDGs) refer directly to education and gender equality:

- achieve universal primary education
- promote gender equality and empower women.

It was hoped that by 2005 gender disparity in education would have been achieved with as many girls as boys going to school. However, this first step was not achieved in over ninety countries and in Niger and Burkina Faso, only one in three girls go to school at all.

CRITICALLY EXAMINE THE RESPONSES TO DEVELOPMENT ISSUES

Multilateral Aid and Bilateral Aid

Multilateral aid is given by multi-national organisations such as the UN, the EU or the AU, benefits from the ability to operate on a large scale and is usually free from ties. Bilateral aid is directly given by one government to another government and is usually related to tied aid.

Tied Aid

Tied aid refers to aid given with conditions attached, usually that the recipient country purchases goods and services from the donor country. Critics of this type of aid say it can lead to higher prices thereby increasing the costs of aid since cheaper goods and services have to be ignored in order to buy from the donor country.

Food Aid

Food Aid provides a short-term immediate solution to a disaster such as famine. However, if allowed to continue in the long term it can present problems for development since countries can become aid dependent. It can also be used by developed countries to dump food surpluses and while this may relieve the situation it can result in local farmers having to compete with free food supplies. Also, corrupt governments can utilise the aid for their own use.

Multilateral Responses

The African Union (AU)

The purposes of the AU are to address the social, economic and political problems faced by many African countries and to accelerate economic development while confronting the problems created by globalisation. The AU regards the promotion of peace, security and stability as a prerequisite for development and it aims to coordinate and intensify cooperation for development within the framework of the United Nations.

The Solemn Declaration (2000) promoted democracy and good governance and the Peace and Security Council addresses regional conflicts. AU peacekeep-

ers have served in Burundi and AU ceasefire monitors were, in 2006, in the western Sudanese region of Darfur, their mandate having been extended from September 2006 until the end of 2006. The AU also oversees the New Partnership for Africa's Development (Nepad), an anti-poverty and pro-development blueprint in partnership with the West. It seeks to promote good political and economic practice in return for more aid and investment.

To help further accelerate economic development the AU helps to coordinate and intensify cooperation between African states and amongst African countries in order to strengthen solidarity and cohesion amongst the peoples of Africa. It further emphasises the importance of meeting the needs of women and young people and has also tackled issues related to HIV/AIDS, malaria and the spread of weapons in Africa.

Criticisms of the AU

Critics of the AU have questioned its leadership, pointing out that many of its leaders are the same people who presided over its predecessor, the Organisation of African Unity (OAU), an organisation that became known as the 'dictators' club'. Moreover, some critics say that, although the AU promotes democracy some AU nations are led by autocrats. Darfur was seen as a key test of the role and effectiveness of the AU. In 2006 it had several thousand troops there in a bid to halt the on-going fighting between rebels and the government and was overseeing a peace deal. Notably, the involvement of the AU in Darfur attracted criticism for being "thin on the ground, poorly equipped and largely symbolic". Finance is another problem. There are doubts about whether the AU, many of whose member nations are struggling to tackle domestic poverty, can afford to fund some of its ambitious schemes.

Department for International Development (DFID)

In July 2006, DFID launched its new White Paper on International Development, Eliminating world poverty: making governance work for the poor. It sets out what the UK government will do to reduce world poverty over the next five years. The White Paper sets out DFID's priorities and explains how it will work with the rest of the UK government, partner governments, international organisations, non-governmental organisations (NGOs), academics and the private sector to fulfil the promises previously made in 2005 to reduce world poverty significantly.

The White Paper's main messages are:
- to increase its development budget to 0.7% of GNI by 2013
- to put good governance at the centre of its work
- to commit 50% of all future bilateral aid to public services for poor people

United Nation Millennium Development Goals (MDGs)

There are eight Millennium Development Goals to be achieved by 2015
- eradicate extreme poverty and hunger
- achieve universal primary education
- promote gender equality and empower women
- reduce infant mortality rates
- improve maternal health
- combat HIV/AIDS, malaria and other diseases
- ensure environmental sustainability
- develop a global partnership for development

However, the Make Poverty History coalition claimed in 2005 that at the current rate of progress:
- halving extreme poverty will not be met until 2147
- universal primary education will not be achieved until 2130
- reducing infant mortality rates by two-thirds will not be met until 2165

United Nations Children's Fund (UNICEF)

UNICEF promotes girls' education ensuring that, as a minimum, they complete primary education. For example, the International Child Friendly Schools for Africa Initiative aims to accelerate access to quality basic education for children, especially girls, in Angola, Malawi, Mozambique, Rwanda and Zimbabwe. It also tries to ensure that all children are immunised against common childhood diseases and are well nourished. Through the 'Unite for Children, Unite against AIDS' campaign it works to prevent the spread of HIV/AIDS among young people and to help children and families affected by HIV/AIDS to live their lives with dignity. UNICEF also upholds the declaration of the Rights of the Child, working to ensure equality for those who are discriminated against, girls and women in particular.

Food and Agriculture Organisation (FAO)

The FAO is a UN organisation which tackles long-term development relating to food. Its mandate is to raise levels of nutrition, improve agricultural productivity and enhance the lives of rural populations. It aims to:
- put information within reach
- share policy expertise (In these two areas the FAO acts as an international point of contact for information and expertise

about all aspects of food production and strategies to tackle food shortages.)

◆ provide a meeting place for nations (for both developed and developing nations to encourage cooperation in tackling food shortages and promoting development)

◆ bring knowledge to the field (managing projects to ensure their success)

World Food Programme (WFP)

The WFP is the UN frontline agency in the fight against global hunger. It tackles short term-food emergencies. It aims to:

◆ save lives in refugee crises and other emergencies

◆ improve the nutrition and quality of life of the world's most vulnerable people at critical times in their lives

◆ enable development by helping people build assets that benefit them directly and promoting the self-reliance of poor people and communities

The WFP provides emergency food in many refugee camps.

WFP and Food Aid—Breaking the Cycle of Poverty

The WFP believes that food aid can help break the cycle of poverty and hunger. Innovative food aid projects, which play an integral part in the WFP's relief, and rehabilitation and development operations, allow the weak and poor to stop worrying about their next meal and build a sustainable future. These include people made homeless by natural disasters, returning refugees, HIV/AIDS orphans and jobless mothers.

WFP and Education

The WFP provides free school lunches as an incentive for the children of poor families to go to school. In 2005, the agency's School Feeding Programme helped 21.7 million children in seventy four countries. Research shows that school feeding can increase attendance by 100% and boost children's performance in the classroom. Pass rates at schools providing free food have invariably gone up. In addition to free lunches, the WFP's take-home rations help to get parents to send their children (boys and girls) to school. In 2005, WFP Djibouti supplied pupils in fifty schools in rural and suburban areas with two meals a day and provided take-home food rations for girls who regularly attended class.

WFP and HIV/AIDS

The WFP uses food aid to soften the blow of HIV/AIDS. The agency distributes its rations to people living with HIV/AIDS so they can provide for their families for longer. This will give them time to transfer vital knowledge and skills to the growing number of AIDS orphans who are the next generation of food providers in developing countries. In Tanzania, under the current Country Programme, the WFP gave household rations to 10,500 food-insecure households affected by HIV/AIDS. This allowed those living with HIV/AIDS to participate in care and treatment programmes and enabled food-insecure orphans to continue attending school.

WFP and Food for Work

The role of the WFP's Food for Work projects is to pay the hungry with food aid to help promote development.

● Food wages give farmers time and energy to build irrigation and terracing to conserve soil and water. In countries where drought regularly causes food shortages, irrigation can boost crop yields by 100 – 400%.

● In war-torn countries, WFP offers food aid as an incentive for soldiers to abandon their weapons and learn new skills.

● Food aid is provided for farmers who practice soil conservation, thereby preventing the overuse of soil and grazing land which in turn helps to reduce desertification.

In Tanzania, Food for Work activities have helped development in the agricultural sector through the participation of over 5,000 households in the construction and rehabilitation of irrigation systems, land rehabilitation and promotion of good post-harvest practices.

Make Poverty History (MPH)

The Make Poverty History coalition called for the unpayable debts of the HIPC countries to be cancelled in full. The G8's debt deal, which had still to be finally agreed by the IMF and World Bank in 2006, should be worth up to $1 billion per year for the eighteen countries that qualify (around twenty more could also become eligible). It also called for a commitment to universal access to HIV/AIDS treatment by 2010 and replenishment of the Global Fund for HIV/AIDS, TB and Malaria. Following this, the G8 countries made a commitment to, as close as possible, ensure "universal access to treatment for all those who need it by 2010".

EUROPEAN UNION (EU)

EU aid is multilateral and financed through the European Development Fund.

Cotonou Agreement

The Cotonou Agreement provides the framework for a twenty-year "partnership for development aid" to seventy seven African, Caribbean and Pacific (ACP) countries, funded mainly by the European Development Fund. The Cotonou Agreement adds a political dimension to ACP-EU "cooperation in development". Agreements relating to peace and security, the arms trade and migration were already in place. Good governance is considered to be a 'fundamental element' of the Agreement with any breaches leading to the partial or complete suspension of development cooperation between the EU and the country involved. The EU is expected to provide 20 billion euros ($18.85 billion) over seven years to ACP countries provided they uphold basic principles of good governance. The new accord also provides for a progressive removal of restrictive trade barriers. In 2008 it will bring in the Economic Partnership Agreements (EPAs) that will replace 'non-reciprocal' trade with 'reciprocal' trade agreements. This will mean that EU exports to ACP countries will be duty free and vice versa.

Key issue:
Assess the effectiveness of Non-governmental organisations (NGOs) in responding to the development needs of African countries.

NON-GOVERNMENTAL ORGANISATIONS (NGOs)

Funded mainly by charitable contributions, NGOs are non-profit, voluntary, formal, non-violent, non-political organisations whose main objective is to promote development and social change by providing relief services and contributing to development projects. However, it should be noted that in some cases NGOs are funded by governments.

NGOs work in partnership with other bodies (donor countries, governments, UN agencies and the EU) to provide both short and long-term aid arguing for small-scale projects, which are locally controlled and sustainable.

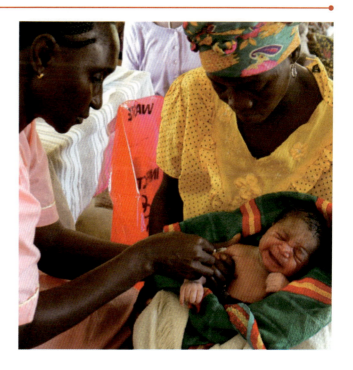

Save the Children

Save the Children concentrates on meeting the needs of children.

In Mozambique, Save the Children UK mainly works in the province of Zambezia, one of the poorest areas of the country. Here it is helping to improve the lives of children and young people, especially the most vulnerable, working to ensure that they have access to good quality basic services. It works in partnership with the government, donors, local and international NGOs, and local communities, as well as with other members of The International Save the Children Alliance.

In Rwanda, Save the Children UK focuses on health care, child protection, and education. In partnership with the local government and community leaders, it has improved the quality of the health service in Gatonde district, and has raised awareness of HIV/AIDS among children. It has also helped children (mostly girls) to return to and stay in school and has helped former child soldiers to return to their villages where it has provided them with education and training so they can earn a living.

Christian Aid

Christian Aid is an agency of the churches in the UK and Ireland which strives to end poverty and injustice through campaigns and education. It works wherever the need is greatest, irrespective of religion or race. It supports local people to find their own solutions to the problems they face.

- Money is not given to governments or individuals
- Funds are channelled into local community groups and church organisations
- The money is then used locally to help in the direct purchase of local commodities
- This encourages the employment of local people
- Christian Aid Week is an annual event of fundraising, prayer and action against global poverty

Actionaid International

Actionaid International is a development agency that fights worldwide poverty through working in partnership with locals to make the most of their own knowledge and experience. Its partners range from small community support groups to national alliances and international networks which together work for better access to education, fair trade and action against HIV/AIDS.

- Through its connections with national and international campaign networks it has been able to highlight the issues that affect poor people and influence the way governments and international institutions think.
- Actionaid's message on food security, trade and HIV/AIDS was highlighted at the Africa Social Forum and World Social Forum in 2003.
- It set up a southern Africa partnership programme to represent ActionAid at meetings of key regional bodies such as NEPAD and teamed up with SEATINI (Southern and Eastern African Trade Information and Negotiations Institute), the African Women's Economic Policy Network and the Africa Leadership Forum in a project aimed at strengthening Africa-based think tanks.

Sample answers to exam questions

To what extent are PR systems more democratic than first-past-the-post? (15)

Answer written by Ryan

The Additional Member System (AMS) is a form of proportional representation and in some ways is more democratic than first-past-the-post (FPTP). This hybrid system is used in the Scottish Parliament and has shown that it provides much more proportional results than the traditional first-past-the-post majoritarian system and therefore reduces wasted votes.

The first part of the AMS is first-past-the-post and provides the traditional results with wasted votes due to the "winner takes all" aspect of this system. However, this is evened up by the second part of the vote which is the list system. This is "pure" PR as the percentage of votes relates directly to the number of seats.

It gives smaller parties the chance to win votes they would otherwise not win as voters can vote for their first choice in the first part of the vote.

For example, the Green Party has 5 MSPs, all elected from the 'party list' part of the voting system. This is fair because some voters would like to have a Green MSP and it is unlikely there are enough Green voters concentrated in any one area.

Some of the larger parties believe that this is undemocratic as it disadvantages them twice; if they do not win in the first section and lose that person's vote in the second part they will be under-represented by the results.

Labour and the Liberal Democrats have recently called for the system to be changed due to this undemocratic element of the system.

It could also be argued that the second part of the system is undemocratic with the List system removing accountability and the link between the voter and the representative.

The listing of candidates means accountability is lost completely as, if a candidate is placed high enough up the list they are elected, whether the public wants them or not.

The additional member system makes the parliament more democratic, but FPTP would be easy to defeat on this front. At the 2005 UK general election, Labour won a majority for five years with only 35% of the total vote across the country.

However, the AMS is a hybrid system which includes the undemocratic system we have in parliament today. This is why some people believe the Single Transferable Vote system (STV) is more democratic.

Marker's comments

Good opening paragraph, which addresses the question: "in some ways is more democratic than first-past-the-post".

Strictly speaking, this is not actually how the AMS works, but the question is not asking how the AMS works. This is a common error. Many students waste time writing descriptive explanations of how voting systems work. Ryan has not wasted too much time here, but he is not scoring any marks either.

These are good paragraphs. They contain detailed, relevant exemplification which answers the question. Ok, so the Greens actually had seven MSPs in the 2003–2007 Scottish Parliament, but Ryan clearly understands the political issue at stake, which is what this question is about.

Fair point, and Ryan is now introducing some balance into the answer. Maybe the AMS is not so democratic after all. It would have been good if he had used this form of words. It is always good practice to use the words contained in the question in your answers!

A bit exaggerated to say "they are elected whether the public wants them or not" as some voters must have voted for them, but the undemocratic party list is a genuine concern about the AMS. Popularity with the 'party machine' is, arguably, more important than popularity with the voters. An example here of well-known MSPs, such as the SNP's Mike Russell, being moved down the party list and losing his seat as a result, would have been good.

Great analysis and exemplification.

Good. It is important to examine more than one system of PR. There is no excuse for not knowing about the STV these days.

STV is used in Ireland and will be used in Scotland for local council elections from 2007. In STV, voters get to list their preferences, rather than putting a simple 'X'. So, a voter gets to vote more than once and doesn't have to choose between parties.

STV is claimed to be more democratic because the voter has more choice. Under FPTP, the voter only has one vote and if the voter likes the party, but doesn't like the candidate, he/she has a problem.

Now, under STV, the voter can, for example, vote for one Labour candidate and not vote for the other one. The voter can spread his preferences around, or just vote for the one party with all his preferences.

STV therefore gives power to the voter, not the political parties. Under FPTP, the big parties have "safe seats" and can stand candidates who may not be very talented. Under STV, the voter has more power and puts pressure on MPs to be more accountable.

STV is clearly much more democratic than FPTP although, like all voting systems, it is not perfect. It could lead to a coalition which no voter voted for and this is a problem which often happens with PR.

To what extent is there a link between income and health?   (15)

Answer written by Chloe

The extent to which there is a link between income and health is that if a person has a low income then they are bound to have poor health as they maybe cannot afford medical treatment. Also, having a low income is clearly linked to high stress levels.

> *Bit strong on class stereotypes here! There is no evidence to back this claim up. Also, despite its faults, we do still have an NHS available to treat people without asking for money. Not a lot of credit in this first paragraph.*

Another link between income and health is the fact that people who are at the lowest end of the social spectrum are the largest consumers of 'junk food'. This means that they get the maximum amount of calories for their money. This therefore leads to health problems such as obesity as they are not gaining vital vitamins etc. to stay healthy.

> *Yes, there is a link between eating junk food and obesity, but Chloe has not answered the question yet. She has still to prove or disprove a link between income and health.*

A third reason which illustrates the extent to which there is a link between income and health is that those who are better off can afford to go on diets and spend money on leisure activities.

Along with this middle classes are more likely to consult health professionals and they will also know how to get the best out of the system and can follow health promotions.

> *It is not good practice to write lines such as "it is also a known fact". Chloe should give evidence of higher rates of smoking among lower income groups. The middle classes are more likely to follow health promotion advice and their better educational levels mean that middle-class groups are more likely to be informed of issues relating to healthy lifestyles.*

It is also a known fact that a higher percentage of those who smoke have lower incomes compared with middle-class citizens.

A major factor amongst those who are better off than others is that they have the option of having private health care.

> *This is true. Chloe could have made much more of this point! She could have developed it, especially by referring to dentistry, where there is a huge shortage of NHS dental care. Those who can afford it take out insurance plans with dentists in the private sector. This leads to inequalities between rich and poor.*

A common problem for many people in the UK is obesity. This is a larger problem for those in lower social classes. For example there are twice as many women in the bottom social class who are obese compared with those in the higher social classes.

> *Chloe clearly knows this issue. She is right to point out that "there are twice as many women in the bottom social class who are obese compared with those in the higher social classes".*

In conclusion there is a significant extent to which income and health are linked through things such as having a low income or being unemployed. I think the lower the income the poorer the health of a person although this does not apply to everyone.

> *Chloe has failed this question, which is a shame. Apart from vague descriptions and a lack of development, there is little or no analysis in Chloe's answer. She attempts analysis right at the end, by saying "in conclusion there is a significant extent to which income and health are linked", but she does not take this further! Her analysis is an 'add on' at the end which does not in fact offer any conclusions at all. This is a common mistake. Really good answers should have conclusions all the way through, rather than a 'conclusion' (which is often a summing up, rather than a conclusion) at the end.*
>
> *Chloe should have debated the issue of whether there is a link between income and health. To some extent yes, but on the other hand, no.*
> - *Yes, poverty is a main contributor to low life expectancy. The Scottish Executive accepts the link between poverty and poor health and has targeted low income communities with resources to improve healthy eating and exercise.*
> - *However, many wealthier people suffer from poor eating habits too. Binge drinking is growing, especially among women of all social classes. Obesity is a problem for all social classes.*
> - *The pressure to buy junk food may be greater for low income groups, but many young people from well-off backgrounds choose unhealthy eating and drinking habits too.*
>
> *All these issues, and more, could have been teased out by Chloe, but her essay was descriptive, rather than analytical. Chloe obviously understands the issues and there is clearly the potential to pass here, but she has to change her essay style to have more balance and to evaluate other points of view.*

Paper Two Good Practice
Decision Making Exercise

SHORT QUESTIONS

Use only the sources. Answer the question directly. Do not 'waffle' or include any extra information. Your answers should be short and straight to the point.

THE DECISION MAKING REPORT

There is not one specified way to write a report. However, a structure is vital and we would recommend this template:

- Introduction
- Arguments for your decision
- Arguments against your decision
- Rebuttal
- Conclusion

The actual topic of the report can come from any aspect of Study Theme 2, Social Issues in the UK. You cannot accurately predict what the topic will be. However, you do not need to as it is primarily skills based. You need to use the source material provided, both textual and statistical.

You then need to supplement this information from your own knowledge of issues in Modern Studies. This is called background knowledge. It must be relevant to your decision and must be facts that have been in the public domain in newspapers or on television or radio.

Background knowledge should permeate your report. There should be little nuggets of knowledge scattered in appropriate places all through your report. This is better than inserting it at the beginning, which always comes across as a bit artificial.

You need to argue a logical case for your decision. You need to be decisive, but you also need to be balanced. Explain the opposing views, but do not be too balanced. Good reports have a rebuttal where you tackle the opposing views and explain why your decision remains the better one. This is not necessarily perfect, but it is the best option.

There follows an example of how to tackle a Decision Making Exercise correctly in order to achieve full marks.

Do the short questions before writing your report. One of the purposes of the short questions is to familiarise you with the source material. So, by the time you come to plan your report, you should be familiar with the key arguments and you should also understand the statistical tables.

We have one suggestion here that you may wish to consider. Background knowledge is an issue for many students. Sometimes students think the background knowledge has to be about the specific task they have been asked to make a decision about. This is not so. You are asked to provide appropriate background knowledge. This can come from any part of Social Issues, or indeed Political or International Issues, so long as the background knowledge is relevant to your argument and the knowledge is in the public domain.

Perhaps before you look at the task in front of you, you might like to think back to the issues you wrote about in your Social Issues essay in Paper 1.

Inequalities in society? Government policies? Opposition policies? Controversial issues in the news? What social issues are the issues of modern times?

Brainstorm. Write them all down in your answer booklet. They may be appropriate to the task. Some may not be relevant, but at least you have something to build on. You do have background knowledge. Write it down while it is fresh in your mind.

SOURCE A

Empower our Disadvantaged Young People

It is important that all our young people are given the chance to achieve their potential. The Scottish Executive has ambitious plans for education. We want Scotland to be the best small country in the world. We have no doubts that a well-educated workforce is the key to economic prosperity for the nation and for individuals.

It is therefore of concern to us that so many of our young people are not in education, employment or training. It is also of concern that our universities continue to be dominated by young people from more privileged backgrounds. They are the children of relatively affluent parents, who themselves have been to university. Pupils from the independent sector, in particular, are much more likely to go into higher education. By contrast, pupils from state schools are more likely to get a job than go to university.

We can stick to the status quo of letting universities themselves decide who they admit to their courses. However, this option is not likely to change current inequalities in terms of access. A more proactive approach is required.

Empower would involve universities working with youngsters from schools in deprived areas. Those interested in attending university would go on a weekend access course which would prepare them for university life.

If Empower-nominated pupils narrowly missed their conditional grades in SQA Higher examinations, and places remained on the courses, these would be offered first to Empower students.

University places would not, therefore, be offered randomly to anyone on a waiting list, as is often the case at the moment. Instead, surplus places would be offered to motivated young people who had shown enterprise and commitment by participating in Empower. The vast majority of young Scots want to do work that is interesting and involves working in a team. It is also very important to many young people that this work is highly paid. A university degree is essential to getting that highly paid job. Empower will offer real assistance towards these ambitions.

Empower will offer a 'hand up' to young people from disadvantaged backgrounds. The children of the middle classes have other, unofficial, 'affirmative' forms of help. They have parental guidance. They attend schools with high academic expectations. They have confidence and goals in their lives.

It is very difficult for the Scottish Executive to ensure that these advantages are available to all in society. Empower will go some way to closing the gap between the socially excluded and the socially included.

James McGuire, spokesperson, anti-poverty charity

SOURCE B

Excellence, not discrimination is the answer

Empower is a predictable response from the Scottish Executive in its attempts to end social exclusion. It is well intentioned, but it is unfair on hard-working young people and will not make Scotland a better country.

Undoubtedly, social exclusion has many severe effects, not just on the individuals concerned, but on wider Scottish society. There are large gaps in life expectancy between different parts of the country, and our health, according to indicators such as dental health, is the worst in Europe. It is right that the Scottish Executive should be addressing issues of social exclusion and inequality, but it is going about it the wrong way.

Universities offer conditional places on the basis that if an applicant can achieve at this level, they are likely to pass the course for which they applied. If they cannot achieve these grades it makes sense to assume that they are likely to fail the course they have applied for too. If Empower is introduced, young people from disadvantaged circumstances are being set up to fail. How cruel!

Empower is also unfair on young people, not necessarily the children of millionaires, who have worked hard all year towards their Highers. They, and their parents, will be very angry when they find out someone with fewer qualifications has been accepted for a course in their place.

Empower also does not understand the role of universities. Universities create the next generation of professionals; our doctors, nurses, teachers and architects. If you go into hospital, you want to be treated by the best. You do not want to be treated by someone the government feels sorry for.

Empower is political correctness gone mad and is insulting to the many children from difficult backgrounds who have made it to university and gone on to be a great success. It is the latest, predictable response to a social problem from the Scottish Executive. It always believes it knows best. Individuals do not have to take responsibility, the government will do it for them. Universities should not be made the scapegoats for society's failings.

Lisa Kirk, newspaper columnist

Source C1

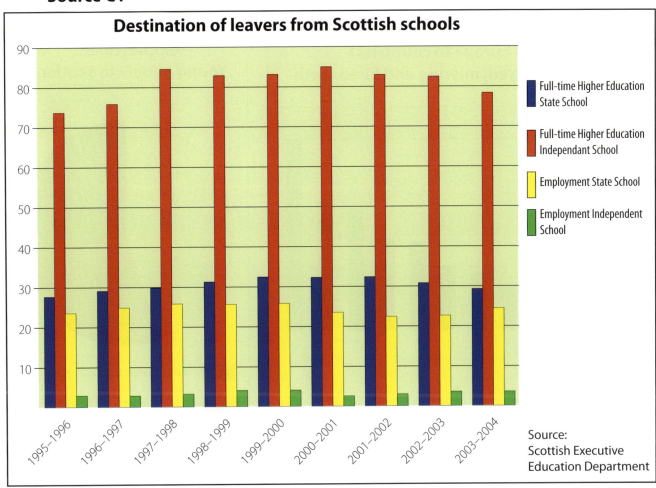

Destination of leavers from Scottish schools

Legend:
- Full-time Higher Education State School
- Full-time Higher Education Independant School
- Employment State School
- Employment Independent School

Source:
Scottish Executive
Education Department

Source C2(a)

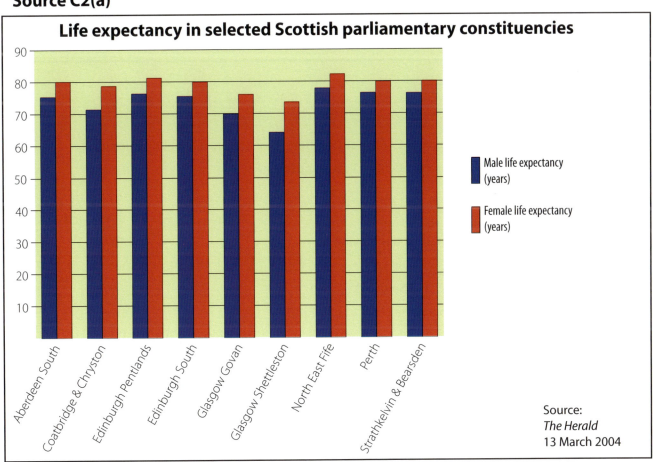

Life expectancy in selected Scottish parliamentary constituencies

Legend:
- Male life expectancy (years)
- Female life expectancy (years)

Source:
The Herald
13 March 2004

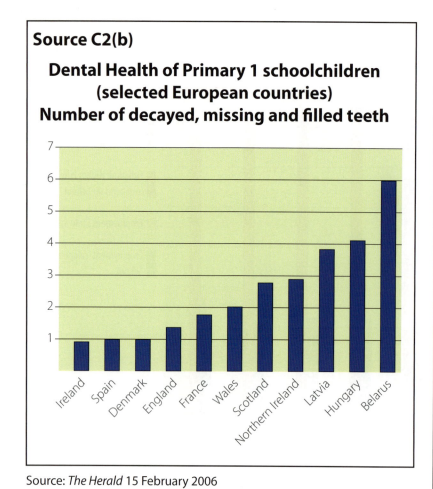

Source C2(b)

Dental Health of Primary 1 schoolchildren (selected European countries)
Number of decayed, missing and filled teeth

Source: *The Herald* 15 February 2006

Source C3

Attitude towards employment: Young people in Scotland

6%

45%

21%

28%

■ More important to be highly paid

■ More important to find the work interesting

☐ More important to work with a team of people I get on with

■ More imortant to work alone as my own boss

Source: Youthlink

DECISION MAKING EXERCISE

QUESTIONS

Questions 1 to 3 are based on Sources A to C. Answer Questions 1 to 3 before attempting Question 4.

In Questions 1 to 3, use only the Sources described in each question.

Question 1
Use only Source C1 and Source A.

Give evidence for and against the view of James McGuire. (2)

Question 2
Use only Source C2 (a), Source C2 (b) and Source B.

To what extent does the evidence support the views of Lisa Kirk? (4)

Question 3
Use only Source C3 and Source A.

To what extent has James McGuire been selective in his use of facts? (4)

Total (10)

Answers
The following is an 'A' quality decision making report.

Question 1

In Source A, James McGuire claims that "Pupils from the independent sector, in particular, are much more likely to go into higher education. By contrast, pupils from publicly funded schools are more likely to get a job than go to university".

It is always good practice to 'lift' the text from the source in your answer.

He is correct that pupils from independent schools are more likely to go to university, as Source C1 shows us that around 80% of these pupils usually go to university, compared to about 30% of state school pupils.

Evidence for his view is correctly identified.

However, he is wrong when he says that pupils from publicly funded schools are more likely to get a job as the numbers entering higher education are greater than those going straight into a job.

Evidence against his view correctly identified. Full marks 2/2. The question is succinctly answered.

Question 2

Lisa Kirk claims that "Undoubtedly, social exclusion has many severe effects, not just on the individuals concerned, but on wider Scottish society. There are large gaps in life expectancy between different parts of the country, and our health, according to indicators such as dental health, is the worst in Europe".

Question 2 is a more difficult question. You are asked to evaluate the extent to which the evidence supports the view of Lisa Kirk. First, what is her view? Correct!

She is wrong when she says that Scotland has the worst dental health in Europe as, while our figures are bad, we are not the worst. Source C2 (b) shows that Belarus has the worst dental health record.

Correct evidence provided. Lisa Kirk is wrong here, correctly identified.

She is right when she talks about life expectancy as Source C2 (a) shows that life expectancy is mid-60s for men in Shettleston, Glasgow yet mid to high 70s in North East Fife.

Correct evidence provided. Lisa Kirk is correct.

To a large extent, the evidence supports her view that social exclusion has severe effects. There are large gaps in life expectancy between rich and poor areas and while our dental health record is not the worst in Europe, it could be a lot better.

It is vital that this conclusion is added. Full marks are unlikely to be awarded unless the 'to what extent' question is addressed. 4/4.

Question 3

James McGuire claims that "The vast majority of young Scots want to do work that is interesting and involves working in a team. It is also very important to many young people that this work is highly paid."

Correctly identified viewpoint from Source A.

To a great extent the evidence supports his view. 45% of young people in Scotland want to work in a team and 28% of young people feel that it is more important for the work to be interesting.

However, he is wrong when he claims that it is very important to many that the work is highly paid as only 21% selected this to be the most important.

Conclusion drawn. The evidence does mostly support his view, but not entirely. Being highly paid is not the most important thing for young Scots according to this survey. This has been identified correctly to gain full marks. 4/4.

Report

Question 4

DECISION MAKING TASK

You are an adviser to the Minister for Education and Young People at the Scottish Executive. You are asked to prepare a report in which you recommend or reject 'Empower' – a proposal to allow Scottish universities to set aside a number of places for students from disadvantaged backgrounds.

Your answer should be written in a style appropriate to a *report*.

Your report should:

- recommend or reject the proposal to introduce Empower
- provide arguments to support your decision
- identify and comment on any arguments which may be presented by those who oppose your decision
- refer to all the Sources provided

AND
- must include relevant background knowledge.

The written and statistical sources which have been provided are:

SOURCE A: Empower our disadvantaged young people
SOURCE B: Excellence, not discrimination is the answer
SOURCE C: Statistical Information

Marker's comments

Introduction

Memo to Minister for Education and Young People by Lianne

I have been asked to recommend or reject 'Empower', a proposal which would allow Scottish universities to set aside a number of places for students from disadvantaged backgrounds.

Read over all the sources. A highlighter pen is handy. Make your plan. Bullet point your key arguments. Plan where your Background Knowledge can be slotted in. Give yourself about 10 minutes to do this, then start writing.

This is a controversial area, but social exclusion is a serious problem in Scotland and something needs to be done to help young people from poorer families have ◄ achievable goals in life. **I therefore recommend the proposal to you.**

State your recommendation right at the beginning.

Reasons for

Scotland is a very unequal country. Inequality touches every part of our lives. As Source C2(a) shows us, people living in deprived communities have much more ◄ unhealthy lives than people in better off areas.

When you refer to a source, identify it to the marker. Using the sources is vital. It is a good idea to write the source used in the margin of your answer paper. Make the marker's job easy! This is a strong argument, good use of the evidence.

Men in Glasgow Shettleston, for example, have a life expectancy in the mid 60s. This contrasts with well-off areas such as Bearsden, where the average man can expect to live into his late 70s. This gap is surely unacceptable.

Something must be going on in poor areas which makes people who live there turn to alcohol. They also turn to cigarettes and drugs more easily. These are coping mechanisms to take them away from the stress of living in poverty.

Crime is also a major problem in poor communities. Many ASBOs have been given out to young people on housing estates (BK) and the Scottish Executive has had a big campaign against knife carrying (BK). Something must be done ◄ to offer a positive alternative to crime and unhealthy living. That alternative is Empower.

Excellent Background Knowledge. Relevant. Appropriate. In the public domain. Write 'BK' in the margin when you have inserted some.

As Source A states, "a more proactive approach is required". This is not a 'nanny state' approach (BK) but simply responsible government.

It is good practice to 'lift' selected quotes from the sources.

Empower is fair. Places on courses will not be offered to people who could not cope. They will be offered to young people who have only just missed the cut-off. These young people will have shown commitment to Empower by attending a weekend course. They will also be ready for university life because, as Source A states, the universities will have come into schools and encouraged the young people before they leave.

It could also be the case that these young people will be desperate to learn and to be a success in life. Source C1 shows us that just about all the pupils from independent schools go on to higher education – almost 80% in 2003–04.

By comparison, only 29% of state school pupils go to university. It can't be the case that these pupils from independent schools are all naturally more intelligent than state school pupils. It must have something to do with the help they get from the private school and also from their well-educated parents.

Good forceful, yet diplomatic, argument. Good use of the sources.

All Empower is doing is balancing things up a little bit, in favour of intelligent young people who have worked very hard in difficult circumstances. The peer group pressure, on boys especially, (BK) not to work hard at school can be very strong, so Empower will offer, as Source A says, a "hand up".

Now, go on to look at the opposing views. These cannot be ignored or simply dismissed as nonsense. A great deal of time will have been taken by the examiners to come up with two plausible decisions. Either one can be correct. There is no one 'correct' decision. So, both sides have their good points. You are supposed to be a little undecided inside yourself about which one is better!
The marks lie in the quality with which you use the sources and your knowledge to weigh up the pros and cons of your decision.

Reasons against
I can understand why some people will be opposed to Empower. It is quite similar to the kind of Affirmative Action programmes that have been tried in the USA and in South Africa (BK). These have been very controversial and have led to a lot of bad feeling, and sometimes even court cases (BK). The same could easily happen here.

Very good BK. Taken from a very different part of the Modern Studies syllabus, but highly relevant. Use of language is good here, acknowledging that the other side has a fair point.

Lisa Kirk (Source B) also makes a good point that universities should always try to recruit the very best people. If you are buying a house and need a lawyer, you aren't interested in what school that lawyer went to, just that he/she is a good lawyer and can do the job well. So, we should be careful not to allow standards to drop.

Lisa Kirk also brings up the argument of "political correctness gone mad". There are so many examples today of 'politically correct' laws that are well-intentioned, but don't work. For example, under Human Rights laws shopkeepers may not be allowed to use CCTV evidence against shoplifters unless they give their permission! (BK)

BK is permeating this report. Again, Lianne is acknowledging that the opposing view has some merit. Good balance.

Note also that the Examiners insert 'coathangers' to give you help towards background knowledge. These are phrases in the text such as "political correctness gone mad" which are designed to stimulate some background knowledge. Can you spot other 'coathangers'?

She also has a good point in that people should stand on their own two feet and work hard to get to university. As Source C2(b) shows, we have one of the worst dental health records in Europe. No one forces us to neglect our teeth and the government does so many things to help us. The ban on smoking in public places (BK) is the best known of recent examples. Perhaps, like looking after our own health, we should look after our own education a bit more.

Good use of this source. It is used as part of an argument, not just mentioned for the sake of it.

Rebuttal

As I stated in my introduction, this is a complex issue and there are no easy solutions to social exclusion. Empower is not perfect, but despite Lisa Kirk's well-explained opposing arguments, I believe Empower to be the best solution.

Affirmative action has been controversial in the USA and South Africa. Nevertheless, it has allowed many people from disadvantaged backgrounds to have opportunities they would never have had. In any case, students from well-off backgrounds, as James McGuire points out, already have an unofficial affirmative action programme working for them.

In terms of Lisa's point about universities recruiting the best: how do we know they are recruiting the best at the moment? As Source C1 shows, universities take in many people from privileged backgrounds. They have had all the advantages of a private education: small classes, well-behaved pupils, educated parents, confidence. In fact, it must be difficult to fail if you have all this going for you.

Perhaps in accepting more working-class pupils, who have only narrowly missed the cut-offs, the universities might be recruiting even better students as they have had to succeed in the face of many difficulties such as crime and peer pressure (BK).

Political correctness is unpopular but there are many examples which at one time could have been called 'political correctness', but are now accepted ways of doing things. For example, there are laws in place to make sure employers aren't racist or discriminate against pregnant women (BK). Empower is not "political correctness gone mad" but good government: helping people to help themselves.

Lisa Kirk has an excellent point when she calls for people to take more responsibility for their lives. This is very much New Labour's approach to the welfare state (BK). However, signing up for Empower, meeting up with universities and going on an access course, is this not taking responsibility? There are plenty of other things teenagers could do at the weekend than go to a university!

Conclusion

The arguments in favour of Empower are overwhelming. Opposition MSPs may well raise similar points to the ones made by Lisa Kirk but, while these views are likely to be held by many people, they can be answered by the good arguments in favour of Empower.

Scotland's young people are not motivated by money. As source C3 shows, they want to do interesting work which will challenge them and allows them to work in a team. We live in a global economy (BK) in which we need an educated workforce with key skills such as teamworking.

The costs to the taxpayer of Empower are minimal. Students from low income backgrounds will need financial help but this money will come back to the government when they get a well-paid job at the end of their studies. Empower will give all Scots the chance to be educated to the level they are suited for.

Balanced, yet decisive. No easy solutions to social exclusion. Great statement! In what ways is this decision the better one? Can the writer rebut Lisa Kirk's opposing views?

Good point, well made.

This is excellent. Really debates the point, making the case for her point of view.

Note the quality of this rebuttal. It does not dismiss the opposing views out of hand, but considers their respective merits and explains how Empower can overcome these problems.

Something else worth considering is money. Every decision taken by the government involves money. For example, while the Scottish Executive receives most of its funding from a block grant from Westminster, increased spending on education has to mean that the Scottish Executive will spend less on some other public service. It is always creditworthy to have an awareness of financial issues such as knowledge of income tax levels or controversies over badly costed spending projects. These make excellent background knowledge.

20/20. A straight 'A'.

A decisive report which is balanced, but clear in its recommendation, and which uses all the sources and background knowledge in all the right places and in all the right ways.

The structure was sound. Whatever the task, the writer could do a good report as the skills of decision making—evaluating sources, using the sources, being objective and being decisive—apply to any situation.

She will not have written a report as good as this at the first attempt. She will have made mistakes in earlier reports. In these Lianne may have forgotten to use all the sources. She may have used some inappropriate background knowledge or may have forgotten it altogether. She may have been indecisive and allowed her opposing views to sound as convincing as her supporting views.

These are mistakes all students make. The key to improvement is to practice and get quality feedback on your mistakes.